NUBIANS IN EGYPT

Peaceful People

THIS BOOK IS PUBLISHED IN COOPERATION WITH THE SOCIAL RESEARCH CENTER OF THE AMERICAN UNIVERSITY IN CAIRO THROUGH A GRANT FROM THE FORD FOUNDATION.

ethnographic essay by ROBERT A. FERNEA *1932-* (handwritten: ALAN, 1932-)

photographs by GEORG GERSTER

Nubians in Egypt

P E A C E F U L P E O P L E

Notes on Nubian Architecture and Architectural Drawings
by HORST JARITZ

Foreword by Laila Shukry El Hamamsy

Captions by Hamza El Din and Elizabeth Warnock Fernea

Additional Photographs by Abdul Fattah Eid

c/wB

UNIVERSITY OF TEXAS PRESS, AUSTIN AND LONDON

wB

Library of Congress Cataloging in Publication Data

Fernea, Robert Alan, 1932–
    Nubians in Egypt.

    Bibliography: p.
    1. Ethnology—Egypt—Nubia.   2. Nubia—Social life
and customs.   I. Gerster, Georg, 1928–   illus.
II. Title.
DT135.N8F47   916.25′03   73-3078
ISBN 0-292-75504-X

Composition by G&S Typesetters, Austin, Texas
Printing and binding by Benteli AG, Bern, Switzerland

CONTENTS

PLATES

All photographs by Georg Gerster except plates 22, 30, 31, 33, 40, 41, 42, 53, 54, 55, 56, 57, 58, 61, 66, and 78, which are by Abdul Fattah Eid.

FOREWORD

The building of the Aswan High Dam, modern Egypt's ambitious effort to harness the Nile for agricultural and industrial purposes, suddenly focused the attention of the world on Nubia. Even though the dam promised to increase Egypt's arable lands by one-third and to provide much needed electricity for industrial development, it had its cost—the total submersion of Nubian lands. Nubia, stretching from Aswan to Dongola in the Sudan, was to disappear under Lake Nasser, the largest man-made lake in the world.

The impending fate of Nubia brought a reaction of alarm throughout the world. Even though Nubia had rarely been visited by outsiders, it was known to Egyptologists as a land rich in ancient Pharaonic sites, including the unique Abu Simbel temple carved into the sandstone cliffs.

When the plans for the building of the Aswan Dam were finalized in the late 1950's, the urgency of preserving the ancient monuments became very much the concern not only of Egypt, but also of many other countries of the world. With the help of UNESCO and contributions from many nations, plans were made for the rescue of the Abu Simbel temple and other monuments. During the few years in which the dam was being built, people swarmed to Nubia—archaeologists and engineers working against time to preserve the most significant monuments, artists and photographers trying to record the beauty of the disappearing land, and ordinary people from Egypt and elsewhere trying to get a glimpse of Nubia and its monuments before the waters of the High Dam irrevocably changed the landscape.

As impressive as the monuments of Nubia turned out to be, particularly Abu Simbel, it was, however, the beautiful Nubian settlements along both banks of the river that were for many the real discovery. Even to us Egyptians, for whom the Nubian was a very familiar figure, his homeland was a surprise and a revelation. We all knew the Nubians as proud, trustworthy, honest, and meticulous workers, a somewhat aloof people who have their own clubs and coffeehouses as well as a well-defined system of mutual aid. We also knew them to be so well knit and organized that no delinquency or crime had ever been known to result from their migration to the turbulent city to work in restaurants, hotels, or the houses of other Egyptians or resident foreigners —even though some of the men would live for years away from home and family. But the richness and elegance of their culture and the beauty of their homes and of the natural setting in which the Nubians lived was an unknown and could not have been guessed at from any contact with Nubian life in the cities. It was ironical and sad that the impending destruction of Nubia was the occasion for many of us to get to know and appreciate Nubian culture.

In 1960, while a large number of scientific archaeological expeditions were active in Nubia and a government survey of the population was envisaged as a preliminary to their mass resettlement, no serious study of the culture that was on the threshold of major modification and readjustment had yet been planned. When Dr. Robert Fernea, then a member of the Sociology and Anthropology Department of the American University in Cairo, suggested to the

Social Research Center that it undertake a research project on Nubian culture, the idea was immediately welcomed. The project fitted very well with the Center's main objectives—the study of the human implications of planned social and economic change and development and the documentation of various aspects of Egyptian culture.

The ethnological survey of Nubia was launched in 1961, supported by a grant from the Ford Foundation, with Dr. Fernea as its director. The purpose of the project was manifold: (a) to record Nubian culture as it had developed over the centuries in its natural habitat; (b) to provide data on the social and economic fabric of Nubian society that might be useful to the planners of resettlement so as to mitigate the stresses of the uprooting; and (c) to obtain baseline data for the future evaluation of the impact of involuntary relocation on Nubian life and thus be able to test some hypotheses relating to social change and adaptation and cultural resistance and resilience.

A number of anthropologists worked on different aspects of Egyptian Nubian culture. Dr. Fernea studied the southern Nubian group, the Fedija; Dr. Charles Callender concentrated on the northern Kenuz living just south of Aswan town; Asaad Nadim and Nawal Nadim collected data on the Arabic-speaking Nubians in middle Nubia—Wadi el-Arab. Dr. John Kennedy worked in Dar el-Salam, a village north of Aswan where Nubians had settled themselves when the first Aswan Dam was built and flooded the land of the Kenuz nearest the dam; Dr. Peter Geiser worked on the adjustment of Nubian migrants to urban life in Cairo.

As the Nubian study constituted the largest project of the Social Research Center in the early sixties, most of the staff of the Center (administrative, research, and secretarial) was mobilized to serve it. The results have been very much worth the effort.

In addition to the present volume, several publications on the Nubians have appeared or are about to do so. *Contemporary Egyptian Nubia*, with Dr. Fernea as editor, was published by Human Area Relations Files, Inc., New Haven, in 1966, and *Life Crisis Rituals among the Kenuz*, by Charles Callender and Fadwa El Guindi, was issued by Case Western Reserve University in 1971. "From Old to New Homeland: A Study of Nubian Resettlement in Egypt," by Dr. Hussein Fahim, is currently in preparation for publication, and a community study by John Kennedy of a previously resettled Nubian village is now ready for publication.

The Social Research Center staff, under the direction of Dr. Hussein Fahim, is now trying to study Nubian life in its new environment. The researchers have already discovered the amazing ingenuity of the Nubians, who, in spite of a lingering sadness for the loss of their traditional home, are taking full advantage of whatever new resources have been made available to them—the schools, the health facilities, the rich new land.

Even though nothing can really compensate for the losses they have suffered, it is hoped that this volume, in trying to recapture and present to the world in word and picture some of the important features of traditional Nubian life, can offer a little consolation to the people of Nubia. The Social Research Center hopes to present in the near future another volume of Nubian life after resettlement as a tribute to a culture that endows its creatures with such inner richness that they can maintain spiritual harmony and create beauty around them with the most meager of material resources.

Laila Shukry El Hamamsy

Director, Social Research Center
American University in Cairo

ACKNOWLEDGMENTS

The work of the Nubian Ethnological Survey would not have been possible without the understanding, help, and guidance provided by Dr. Laila Shukry El Hamamsy, director of the Social Research Center, American University in Cairo, and John Hilliard, then the Ford Foundation representative in Egypt. Many other people in Egypt at that time helped to facilitate our research, most especially Lewa Mohammed Safwat, then deputy undersecretary in the Ministry of Social Affairs, which had much of the responsibility for the gigantic task of resettling the more than fifty thousand Egyptian Nubians. The late social anthropologist Francisco Benet, then social science representative of UNESCO in Egypt, also provided much encouragement and friendship.

Scholars and researchers who shared the work of the Nubian Ethnological Survey were Mohammed Fikry Abdul Wahab, Charles Callender, Karim Durzi, Bahiga Haikal El Ghamry, Abdul Hamid El Zein, Hussein Fahim, Peter Geiser, Afaf El Deeb Henein, Samiha El Katsha, John G. Kennedy, Sohair Mehanna, Omar Miselemi, Asaad Nadim, Nawal El Messiri Nadim, Aziza Rashad, Fadwa El Guindi Rosenbaum, Thayer Scudder, and Nadia Haggag Youssef, as well as Najwa Shukairy, whose master's thesis became part of the Nubian record. Without their interest and enthusiasm, most knowledge of Egyptian Nubian life before resettlement would now be limited to the memories of the Nubians. The essay that follows grew out of my own research and residence among the Nubians; while it is my own responsibility, the ideas of all those who worked with me in Nubian villages and studied Nubian migrants in the cities of Egypt have greatly contributed to my understanding. I can only thank them as a group for their cooperation and friendship.

Anthropologist William Y. Adams, who will soon publish his own study of Nubian history, kindly read Chapters 2 and 3 of this book before publication. His knowledge of published and unpublished evidence made his comments extremely helpful. Historian John A. Williams also read these chapters critically and made valuable suggestions. However, any errors of fact or interpretation are my own.

Dr. Georg Gerster, Swiss scholar, photographer, and journalist, has also written a study of Nubian history. His willingness to become a partner in this effort grew out of his admiration for the communities of modern Nubia, which he came to know and photograph during his studies of Nubian antiquities.

During the course of our studies, each of us came to have special friends among the Nubians who devoted many hours of their time to our education. Their willingness to help us and the general warmth of Nubian hospitality made our work among the Nubians a great pleasure. I hope that this book is some measure of our appreciation.

I owe a special debt of gratitude also to Hamza El Din, Nubian musician and composer, and my wife, Elizabeth W. Fernea, who selected and captioned the photographs together. Hamza shared with us the determination that a glimpse of the life and history of his people should be available to those who had no opportunity to visit his ancestral homeland.

Robert A. Fernea

NUBIANS IN EGYPT

Peaceful People

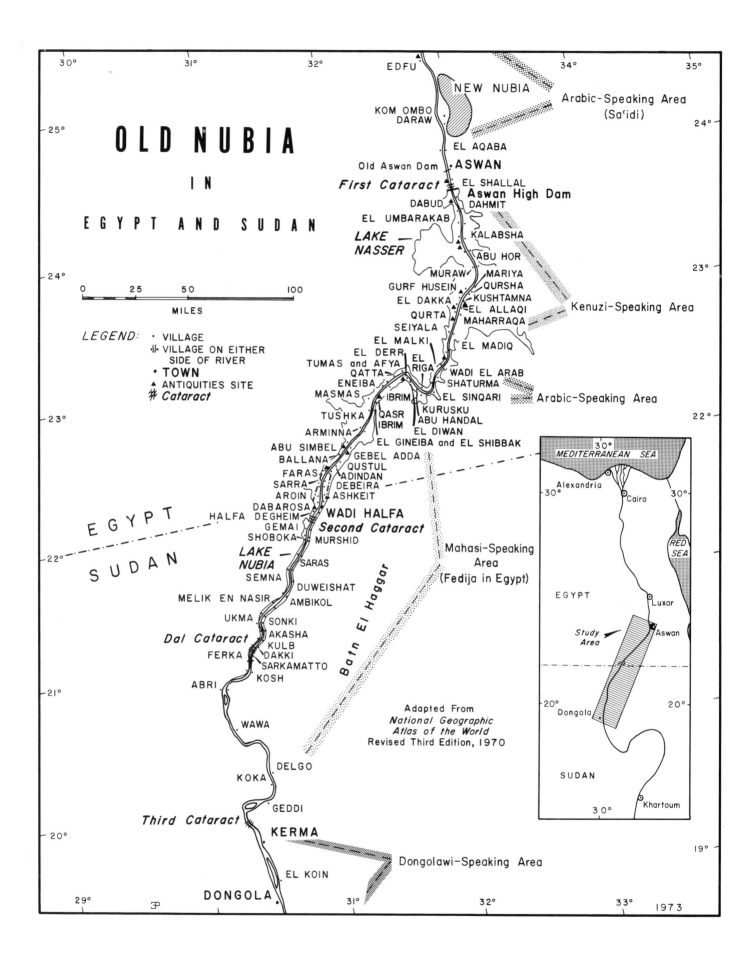

OLD NUBIA
IN
EGYPT AND SUDAN

SCALE
0   25   50   100
MILES

LEGEND:
- • VILLAGE
- ⑊ VILLAGE ON EITHER SIDE OF RIVER
- • TOWN
- ▲ ANTIQUITIES SITE
- ⑊ Cataract

EDFU
NEW NUBIA
Arabic-Speaking Area (Saʿidi)

KOM OMBO
DARAW
EL AQABA
Old Aswan Dam   ASWAN
First Cataract   EL SHALLAL
Aswan High Dam
DABUD   DAHMIT
EL UMBARAKAB
KALABSHA
LAKE NASSER
ABU HOR
MURAW   MARIYA
GURF HUSEIN   QURSHA
EL DAKKA   KUSHTAMNA
QURTA   EL ALLAQI
MAHARRAQA
SEIYALA
EL MALKI   EL MADIQ
EL DERR
TUMAS and AFYA   EL RIGA
QATTA   WADI EL ARAB
ENEIBA   SHATURMA
MASMAS   IBRIM   EL SINQARI
KURUSKU
TUSHKA   QASR   ABU HANDAL
IBRIM
ARMINNA   EL DIWAN
ABU SIMBEL   EL GINEIBA and EL SHIBBAK
BALLANA   GEBEL ADDA
FARAS   QUSTUL
SARRA   ADINDAN
AROIN   DEBEIRA
DABAROSA   ASHKEIT
HALFA   DEGHEIM   WADI HALFA
GEMAI   Second Cataract
SHOBOKA   MURSHID
LAKE NUBIA   SARAS
SEMNA
MELIK EN NASIR   DUWEISHAT
AMBIKOL
UKMA   SONKI
Dal Cataract   AKASHA
KULB
FERKA   DAKKI
SARKAMATTO
ABRI   KOSH

Arabic-Speaking Area

Kenuzi-Speaking Area

Mahasi-Speaking Area (Fedija in Egypt)

Batn El Haggar

EGYPT
SUDAN

WAWA

DELGO
KOKA
GEDDI
Third Cataract   KERMA

EL KOIN
DONGOLA

Dongolawi-Speaking Area

Adapted From
National Geographic Atlas of the World
Revised Third Edition, 1970

MEDITERRANEAN SEA
Alexandria
Cairo
RED SEA
EGYPT
Luxor
Study Area
Aswan
Dongola
SUDAN
Khartoum

1973

1. The Importance of the Nubians

The life of the Nubian people, as described in the following pages, no longer exists. The Egyptian government has resettled the Nubians in new communities and on new lands north of the city of Aswan, near Kom Ombo. Waters of the Nile, backed up by the High Dam at Aswan, have covered the houses and flooded the area where these people lived hundreds, perhaps thousands, of years. Yet Nubian culture, developed during a long history, has not been obliterated by the floodwaters. The values and techniques that allowed Nubians to live peacefully in a difficult environment in the past still persist to some extent in the new communities, helping these people adjust to radically different patterns of life. As we shall see, the building of the High Dam and the resettlement of Nubian villagers are only the most recent of a long series of events that have brought Nubians ever more into the mainstream of Egyptian society. In a world in which people are constantly being uprooted from their native communities, and where their traditional culture seems of little use in their new settings, the Nubian example is worthy of our attention.

Like the Nubians, most of mankind lived during the greater part of history in small, relatively isolated settlements and villages and slowly developed workable variations on the basic themes of human culture. Today the isolation necessary for such creativity is largely gone, and distinctive small communities themselves are vanishing, if not under the floodwaters of the Nile, then at least in the homogeneous mixture we call modern society. Little record remains of the achievements of many of the cultures that have already disappeared: achievements in terms of values; patterns of social relations; techniques for wresting subsistence from varying environments; approaches to expression and communication in pictorial art, in words, in the building of houses, and in the fashioning of the objects of everyday life. These unique manifestations of human capabilities will not appear again, and we are all poorer for their loss. This book is an attempt, then, to record some of the achievements of the Nubian people while they still lived in their ancestral home.

Who are the Nubians? Western readers may recall that the Nubian is mentioned in histories of Pharaonic Egypt, both as king and slave, and also appears as a character in the tales of the *Arabian Nights*. The foreign visitor to modern Cairo will be told that the tall, elegantly garbed black employees

3

in the best hotels are Nubians, urban migrants from villages in the southernmost region of Egypt who are famous for honesty and faithful service. But such fragments of knowledge scarcely answer our basic query. To discover who the Nubians are, we must look both to the past and to the present of this ancient population of Middle Eastern people, a people who share much of their heritage with other residents of the Nile valley, but who have retained to the present day a rich cultural tradition that is uniquely their own.

In general, the people called Nubians are those whose native villages extended along the Nile from the first cataract at Aswan south into the Sudan through the region known as Dongola. Because of Nubia's unique position between two competing centers of power, her exact boundaries have never remained fixed. The present border between Egypt and the Sudan, which splits Nubia and divides the population, is the most recent outcome of this situation. Within Nubia itself, several distinct groups of peoples may be identified. Nubians speak two related languages in several localized dialects, and some other social and cultural differences are to be found among the inhabitants of this thousand miles of Nile shoreline.

Historically, the Nubian region has been both an isolated stretch of Nilotic villages and a continuously settled area of land linking sub-Saharan Africa and Egypt. In this unusual combination of circumstances lie many factors that help explain the development and persistence of this special group of people. Nubia, because of its often inhospitable desert environment and limited natural resources, has never become a traffic corridor or a mere zone of transition between Egypt and Africa. River traffic has always been discontinuous, impeded by long, impassable stretches along this section of the Nile and a shore line cut by rocky cliffs and water-filled ravines.

The relative poverty and isolation of the region discouraged colonialism and encouraged indigenous cultural development. Foreigners visited or invaded Nubia from time to time, as soldiers, administrators, and raiders; some married Nubian women, but until recently, when such intermarriage took place, the outsider was more likely to settle in the village community, than to take his bride out of Nubia. Thus, whatever the origins of the foreign fathers, the children of these unions grew up learning Nubian languages and customs. Contact with the outside world remained sporadic, and, as centuries passed, the small number of outsiders was each time gradually absorbed into the local communities.

Thus, the question of Nubian identity in a physical or a genetic sense is as complex as the question of their cultural heritage. Their physical appearance, as a tall dark-skinned people of proud bearing, remains distinctive in Egypt, however, despite their many resemblances to the people of Africa, the Mediterranean world, and the surrounding desert. Though in Sudan the Nubians cannot readily be distinguished from their other Muslim neighbors, in Egypt today the term Nubian still continues to refer to a black minority in the cities who come from a particular region of the country. Today, as we shall see in succeeding chapters, in spite of differences among themselves the Nubians' own sense of their identity is strong.

Like their American counterparts, the Nubians have had to struggle to overcome not only the disadvantages of rural origins but also the social stigma of historical involvements with slavery, involvements that for both groups finally ended in the nineteenth century. Both Nubians and American blacks have been victims of uncomplimentary references and stereotypic attitudes on the part of some of their numerically superior fellow citizens.

But the obvious comparison between these two minority groups must not be overdrawn. The persistence of exclusively Nubian villages, repositories of a distinct culture, has helped this people at all times to retain a sense of who they are. The black American is now attempting to discover a heritage all but obscured by generations of white domination. This is not a Nubian problem. Nor does the modern Nubian face the barrier of discriminatory legislation and racist institutions that have been the lot of American black men. Modern Nubian history is that of Muslims in a largely Muslim society, a society that has never created distinctions within itself through Jim Crow legislation. The Nubian people, without the crippling effects of institutionalized racism, have been able to establish peacefully a place for themselves in Egyptian society. Today Egyptian Nubians compare favorably with the Egyptian society at large by almost every social and economic standard.

The Nubians, like village people everywhere, have been obliged to cope with the problems of a modern world not of their making, a world created and dominated by urban people employing technologies far different from those utilized in small rural communities. For the Nubian population, however, the pressure has been particularly strong and relentless. Since the turn of the century, when the first barrage was constructed at Aswan, the arable lands of the Nubian valley, never plentiful, have been progressively diminished by the reservoirs of ever-higher dams. This steady encroachment culminated with the High Dam at Aswan, which has finally flooded the entire region of Egyptian Nubia and part of Sudan, necessitating the resettlement of those villagers who had not already departed to more prosperous regions of the country. For the first time in many centuries, technology has created an unoccupied zone between Sudan and Egypt; thus, Nubia, as an inhabited region, is now at an end in Egypt and greatly diminished in the Sudan. Nearly a decade has passed since the village Nubians faced the trauma of resettlement in government-built villages south of Aswan, near Kom Ombo, and in Kashim el-Ghurba in the Sudan, and the region we shall be discussing is now under many feet of water.

The sudden and dramatic quality of the Nubians' relocation should not obscure the fact that these people are experiencing, in a more concentrated way, what minorities of people throughout the world have faced: the loss of isolation and cultural independence, which threatens us all with the dreary consequences of uniformity. Traditional cultural differences, those unique variations in the conduct of human life, have for a long time been subject to the irresistible pressures of conforming change; cultural diversity is everywhere rapidly being replaced by the more banal difference of economic class. The effect of mass communication, easy social contacts, and common economic involvements threatens the persistence of all distinctive traditions just as surely as the Aswan High Dam threatened the existence of the Abu Simbel temple and the other monuments of Pharaonic culture in Nubia.

Seen against the larger background, the Nubian achievement has been remarkable. In a few generations, what the Nubians have accomplished is not the sterile preservation of themselves as cultural curiosities (however admirable) but rather a series of social transformations that have sustained their villages and permitted the individual Nubian to find his own footing in the rapidly changing world into which he has been thrust.

The more significant question is not "who are the Nubians" but how have they been able to cope. In 1963, when they were moved to Kom Ombo, the trauma of resettlement was great, and dire predictions were made about the Nubians' future. Yet today, less than fifteen years later, they dominate local elections to the Egyptian National Assembly; their children have demonstrated amazing success in the Aswan public schools; and they have renovated many of the houses provided by the Egyptian government, to make them conform more to Nubian ideas of space and comfort.

What are the particular qualities of Nubian culture that have enabled these people to face, with such courage and success, the change and uprooting to which they have been subject? Is the development of social means of resolving conflict and avoiding violence within their communities the key to their achievement? Has the central position of women as the guardians of cultural continuity provided a special strength? Our book is an effort to challenge, with new myths, the old myths about the Nubians derived from the tales of Scheherazade and the Pharaonic wall paintings. I use the phrase "new myths" advisedly, for Nubian river life of more than a decade ago, like the days of Scheherazade, is now a thing of the past.

The new myths that I will attempt to set forth are based on studies of Nubian history, culture, and society before resettlement. The substance of these new myths hopefully may help us understand some of the problems faced by comparable groups everywhere, perhaps by each of us as we attempt to deal with a world that so little resembles that of our parents.

The increasing loss of cultural, social, and economic autonomy and the often subsequent breakdown of social order that cultural minorities throughout the world have had to face cannot be avoided by creating artificial reservations that lack adequate and appropriate means of subsistence. We know this only too well from the disasters of our national policies toward the American Indians. The Soviet creation of ethnically and linguistically based "states" lacking political and economic autonomy may also prove, in the end, to have been a futile gesture. The problem is not how to avoid change but how we can accept it and survive, not only in the physical sense, but also in terms of the self-respect, sense of personal worth, group identity, and peaceful cooperation with one's fellow man that makes life worthwhile for the individual.

Thus, while the book that follows is a picture of a way of life that has largely ceased to exist since the High Dam was built at Aswan, it is also a study of the cultural heritage of a people who have found ways of adapting to drastically changed conditions of life.

Of course, the key to the Nubians' success is to be found partly in the nature of Egyptian society, which has made many alien minorities a part of itself throughout its long history. But most importantly, the success of the Nubians rests, I believe, upon the nature of their own unique society. What kind of people created Nubian society? This is the central problem to which this essay is addressed. Even if the answer remains partially obscure, it is here we must search to understand something of the conditions necessary to the survival of us all in a changing world, which our plans cannot anticipate nor our minds fully comprehend.

2. The Nubian Past

Over several millennia, Pharaonic, Christian, and Muslim kingdoms rose and fell within or adjacent to the land we call Nubia. But until the middle of the twentieth century, the history of the Nubian people could only be dimly perceived within the chronological events set down in the written records of neighboring states and in the accounts of foreign travelers. Recent archaeological work and research in Arabic archives are now adding new perspectives to this framework, from Pharaonic times to the Christian period (from the sixth to the fifteenth century), and in the later Muslim era.

The many excavations of sites within Nubia that took place before the land was flooded by the Aswan High Dam have yielded a great deal of new information, including written documents, previously unknown, from the Christian period. "The known time range for old Nubian documents is from A.D. 795 to 1484. By far the greatest mass of this material (none of it yet published) has come from Qasr Ibrim; the majority of it is official and private letters, legal documents, and the like. . . . In fact, the material from Ibrim shows clearly that Old Nubian and Arabic were the secular written languages of me-dieval Nubia and were very widely understood, while Coptic and Greek were employed almost exclusively in religious texts."[1]

The Nubians themselves have as their heritage, in addition, an oral history, a rich, undated treasury of artifact and myth. For centuries these people were born and matured in a land filled with the monuments and ruins of past civilizations. Remnants of the Christian and early Muslim eras are part of the landscape, and folk traditions persist from both periods. The more spectacular temples and statuary of Pharaonic times, which have been part of the daily lives of the Nubians for as long as four thousand years, have also been the source of tales and legends. In the twentieth century, the temples partly inspired an architectural renaissance in Egyptian Nubia.

However, this brief historical survey is not designed to claim, for example, that Pharaonic Egypt contributed only archaeological inspiration to modern Nubia, or to indicate what specific influences were added during Christian and Muslim eras. The

[1] William Y. Adams, personal communication.

threads of these historical experiences are woven so tightly into the fabric of contemporary Nubian culture that specific debts to the past can scarcely be identified. We can only examine some known events and conditions and try to infer what might have been the consequences of such events and conditions for the people of the time.

Egyptian Nubia has always been a relatively isolated area, somewhat poor in the resources that might have encouraged permanent colonization for agrarian purposes. The cataract at Aswan was a natural barrier to river traffic long before any dams were built, and the scorching deserts on either side of the narrow Nile valley discouraged both entry into and exit from the settled area. The arable land consisted of small amounts of alluvial soil deposited annually by the Nile. The size of such deposits varied according to the flood, and the soil shifted with the wind and water erosion. Beyond the alluvium lay sterile sand and rock, and the Nubians ventured into this barren area only to bury their dead or to gather the grasses and plants that sprang up spontaneously after an occasional rain.

On the other hand, until Nubia became a Muslim land, it was an important source of slaves for the Middle Eastern world. At different periods in its long history, Nubia also accumulated considerable wealth as an intermediary in trade between African and Mediterrean regions. It was therefore a target for numerous invasions and raids until this century.

The introduction of the water wheel to Nubia in Roman times was a significant contribution to the local economy. In peaceful years, the villagers utilized the water wheel to enlarge the area and extend the period of cultivation. But in troubled times, investments in irrigation equipment and terraced lands were not possible; the Nubians then must have survived by planting quick-growing crops like millet on the riverbanks, crops that could grow while the soil was still damp from the annual flood. The date palm trees brought a spurt of prosperity to some parts of Nubia, but these seem to have been introduced as a source of cash crops only during the nineteenth century. In general, the environment placed ironbound restrictions on the economic growth of the area; it could only provide a subsistence economy for a limited number of people. Given the meager resources, no population centers

of any great size could develop. The entire population of the Nubian valley probably never numbered more than a few hundreds of thousands, and then only when peaceful conditions prevailed.

The conventional histories of this region must be examined, then, with the ecological background in mind. For example, we read that in the sixth century Nubia became a Christian land. The Empress Theodora sent missionaries from Constantinople who converted the local leaders, and shortly thereafter the entire thousand-mile area from Aswan to Dongola was united under one king. This achievement seems almost incredible if, that is, we view the Nubian conversion to Christianity and the subsequent statehood in anything like the modern sense. For, as we have already stated, much of the Nubian region consisted of rocky shore line, and the settlements were sparse and widely separated. The obvious difficulties of communication must have limited considerably the contacts for both administrative and religious purposes. Postrevolutionary Egyptian officials tried, with modern technological means, to "integrate" Nubia into the centralized administration of Egypt. Yet, in 1960, few officials had penetrated this riverine land, and inhabitants of most of the villages could not remember that any outsiders had come to their communities before preparation for resettlement began. Probably, the Nubian communities, linguistically diversified and widely separated, were united and administered only enough to permit the more powerful centers of the region to collect tribute from the weaker, a pattern found elsewhere in the Middle East during this period.

The limited archaeological evidence from Christian times suggests the emergence of a wealthy clerical hierarchy, probably with considerable secular authority. On the walls of the rare Nubian churches found and excavated during the sixties, enormous frescoes were discovered, picturing ecclesiastical figures, dressed in the rich regalia of the Eastern church. Despite eyes somewhat distorted and enlarged according to the iconic style then in favor, the figures are undoubtedly Nubian.

Very likely the church of Theodora's time re-created in Nubia, on a reduced scale, the same hierarchically organized theocratic structure then existing in the Byzantine Empire. The claims of the church on the lives of the Nubians can be inferred from the presence of a few large public buildings, the cost of which would probably have been a burden for the average villager. The importance of the clerical hierarchy may have been limited in the more isolated settlements, yet the contribution of this religion to Nubian culture finds testimony in names, customs, legends, and folk art motifs, which have persisted in contemporary times. Furthermore, the Christian hierarchy of Nubia reinforced a structure for formal leadership and helped give the outside world an authority with which it could deal.

In the seventh century, the new Arab ruler of Egypt, ʿAbdallāh ibn Saʿd, invaded and conquered Nubia. But, instead of pressing the claim of Islam, he quickly withdrew and concluded a treaty with the Christian Nubian king that became the basis for relations between the two regions during the next six hundred years.

According to the treaty, an annual tribute of 350 slaves was sent to Cairo, following the custom in relations between a Muslim state and a subordinate Christian state. In return, the Egyptians were to send gifts to Nubia of food, horses, and cloth, which may well have been an important source of income for those who received and distributed this benefice. The treaty also suggests to us that Nubia was to remain open to Muslim traders, who were not to live there, but for whom a mosque was to be provided. Clearly, it was in the interests of Egypt to have, on its southern border, a friendly, technically independent buffer state with which it could trade.

Islam, however, was an important force in the lives of the Christian Nubians long before the final collapse of the Christian states and the eventual conversion of the population. To the north lay a powerful Muslim neighbor, Egypt, and the nomad tribes in the surrounding deserts were largely Muslims, as well. In the eleventh century, the Rabīʿa, an Arabian tribe from Yemama who had first entered Egypt in the ninth century, forcibly settled in the Nubian region around Aswan, and at this time the first general conversion of a part of the Nubian population is likely to have occurred. The Rabīʿa brought their religion and tribal political organization with them, but they adopted the language and presumably much of the culture of the villagers as, over the years, they intermarried with the local population and came to be called the

Beni Kanz, and later the Kenuz, a name for this group of northern Nubians that survives to this day.[2]

The history books provide no further indications of mass conversion from Christianity to Islam until the final conversion of the local Nubian elite, some five centuries later, made it a matter of official state importance and thus worthy of recording. The Arab historian, Ibn Khaldūn, notes that in the fourteenth century southern Nubians in positions of authority, who needed to consolidate their ties with the more powerful Arab tribes occupying neighboring deserts, married their sisters to Arab sheikhs. In giving their women to the Arabs, says Ibn Khaldūn, the Nubians also gave away their princedoms, since not only did the children of such marriages become Muslims according to Muslim law, but also, according to Nubian custom, titles and lands were passed from sister's brother to sister's son.

If matrilineal inheritance was the Nubian custom in Christian times, the Nubians' vulnerability to Arab domination becomes clearer. Intermarriage, a famous instrument of diplomacy among Arab tribes long before Islam, transformed the Nubians into Muslims without the necessity of full-scale conversion. Again, however, it must be remembered that, whatever the father's origins, the child learns to speak from its mother and begins the discovery of himself generally within her domain. Thus, the southern villages of Fedija Nubians, like their northern Kenuzi neighbors, retained their own language and, we presume, much of their traditional culture. That this culture resembled that of other Nilotic villages more than that of the distant world of Byzantium seems safe to assume. Then, as now, this traditional culture, incorporating whatever elements it may have absorbed from other sources, was transmitted by the women of Nubia, in an almost unbroken sequence, to succeeding generations.

Around the beginning of the sixteenth century, the last Christian Nubian kingdoms passed from recorded history, and our knowledge of the local populations becomes even more limited. The villages of Nubia, lacking any centrally organized diplomacy and with very limited military strength, were left to deal with nomadic populations as best they could. As in

---

[2] Beni Kanz and Kenuz were terms derived from the title "Kanz el-Dawla" bestowed on a chief of this group in late Fatimid times.

other times and places, some of these villages surely placed themselves under the protection of specific tribes and came to be regarded in some instances as settled branches of the same tribal group.

The disappearance of the last active Christian church in Egyptian Nubia is recorded as having occurred during the sixteenth century, though most of the ecclesiastical organization had collapsed before this. Historical studies generally refer to Nubia as an Islamic region by this time. However, conversion to Islam could not at first have been universal, nor did it have uniform results for all Nubians. Chronicles of medieval times show that some Nubians, recognized as Muslims, were listed as free men in the labor forces of Lower Egypt. But at the time, Nubians were also taken in slavery, because they either were not Muslims or were not recognized as such. The northern Kenuzi Nubians would not seem to have been subject to enslavement, because of their earlier conversion and their proximity to Egyptian Muslim influence.

But many Nubian communities, particularly in the south, even if once converted to Islam, had little means of maintaining the practice of their new religion. With the collapse of the church-based administration, no central authority existed that could support local centers of learning, and the occasional presence of alien armed forces must have drained off any economic surpluses the area produced. Without provision for the continual propagation of the religion, conversion meant little to the convert, for Islam, particularly among non-Arabic-speaking people, needs literate men who can read the Quran, lead prayers, and supervise the religious education of the young. Therefore, if any of these Nubians were enslaved by Muslims, it must have been largely because, unable to demonstrate their beliefs, they were not regarded as true Muslims.

The issue of conversion to Islam and recognition as Muslims is thus extremely important to our understanding of the Nubian past, not only because of the great legacy of personal belief and social institutions that Islam provided for the Nubians, but also because recognition as Muslims ended the dangers of enslavement: Islam expressly forbids one Muslim to enslave another Muslim.

As a people, the Nubians were never totally enslaved, and the present generations are for the most part not the descendants of slaves. The latter qualification is needed only because Nubians, no less than other Middle Eastern groups, owned slaves, as part of their household labor forces, while this practice was permitted and when they could afford to do so. As elsewhere, the slaves were absorbed eventually into the population and strengthened the African contribution to the Nubian community. Those Nubians who were themselves unfortunate enough to be taken and enslaved (young boys were preferred) were lost to their villages forever. Often they were castrated, thus eliminating even the possibility of descendants outside Nubia.

But association with slavery, in whatever form, has left a common legacy among Nubians, expressed today in their determination to refute any accusation of inferiority, by demonstrating their devotion to Islam and by striving to advance through the channels of social mobility that are as open to them as to all other Egyptians. For, unlike black Americans, black Egyptians never have had to face the social and economic barriers of racist institutions, which have remained an obstacle to equality of opportunity in the United States long after the institution of slavery was outlawed. Being recognized as Muslim conferred formal equality, and this has had a formative influence on Nubian life in the last century.

The collapse of the Christian states in Nubia and the conversion of the population to Islam coincided with the long period of Mameluke rule in Egypt. The Mamelukes were a military slave elite who ruled Egypt from 1250 to 1517 and then administered it until their power was decisively ended by Mohammed Ali in the early nineteenth century. Relations between Egypt and Nubia during this long period varied between total lack of interest in Nubia to the establishment of military garrisons near the present southern border of Egypt. As we shall see, these garrisons became the basis for new ruling aristocracies in the region. In the final overthrow of the Mamelukes, their survivors fled south, attempting to escape Mohammed Ali, and ravaged many Nubian communities.

Troubled conditions persisted in much of Nubia until the latter part of the nineteenth century. Again, the situation varied, as European travelers of the period have attested. James August St. John

The winter crops grew along the edge of the river, creating a lush strip of green in the desert landscape.

The family water supply came from the Nile, carried up by the women in morning and evening.

Women mixed the newly milled flour with salt and water to make bread, flat thin cakes that were baked daily on large griddles of iron or clay.

Painting on the inside wall of a house courtyard.

traveled in Nubia in 1832, and at some points in his journey up the Nile south of Aswan he found a desperately poor people, living half-naked, in makeshift houses, having been reduced by Mameluke raids, apparently, to the most meager levels of subsistence:

> . . . in all of these villages there is no bread to be obtained. Milk and butter are generally found, however, but these, together with eggs,—when they can be procured—are considerably dearer than in Egypt. . . . [the Nubians] appear, at present, to entertain no hopes of a political change, though the slightest reverses occurring to Mohammed Ali, would again, I make no doubt, awaken their ancient love of anarchical independence. If we assert, with Burckhardt, that the villages of the Nubians are built of stone, a wrong idea of them will certainly be conveyed; yet I scarcely know what other terms to employ. The huts of which they consist are, in many cases, merely so many low circular walls of small loose stones, piled rudely upon each other, and covered above with dhourra [millet] stalks; they are so frail that the smallest force would be sufficient to destroy them. Twelve or thirteen of these huts, often fewer, huddled together among heaps of ancient ruins, or on the shingly slope of the mountains, constitute a village, or hamlet, which might be easily passed without notice, particularly in the dawn or twilight, being exactly of the same hue as the surrounding rocks.[3]

Yet, despite the poverty of the Nubians, St. John records with admiration their industry: in other areas of the country, he notes, "every day we saw fresh proofs of the industrious character of the present inhabitants. The perserverance they exhibit in watering their fields, when prevented by poverty from erecting *sakia*[s] [water wheels in Egyptian Arabic] is exemplary."[4]

The above observation can be contrasted with the description of Nubian activity near Aswan, closer to Egypt, in the area where Islam had been longer established. Just south of the First Cataract near the temple of Philae, St. John reports that he saw the following:

> . . . to enlarge the extent of their fields, the industrious inhabitants construct long walls, or jetties, of large stones, running out at right angles with the banks to a considerable distance into the stream, narrowing its course, and allowing the mud, which

quickly accumulates behind them, to harden into solid land, which is immediately brought into cultivation. I have observed a similar practice on a smaller scale, upon the banks of the Rhone, in the Upper Valais; where, in fact, much land might thus be gained, had the Valaisans half the industry and energy of the Nubians. The skill, neatness and enterprise of these people, who, having for ages enjoyed more freedom, are superior in vigour and hardihood to the Fellahs, excited our admiration.[5]

As he moved once more farther south, into the Fedija area, St. John noted still other developments:

> The inhabitants of Derr are supposed to be the descendants of a number of Bosnian soldiers, established in Nubia by the Sultan Selym; and still in a great measure preserve their comparatively fair complexion and European features, though in many instances, it is clear, from their physiognomy, they have intermarried with blacks. In the morning several decently dressed lads passed by our boat on their way to school, with the wooden tablets, on which they are taught to write, in their hands.[6]

The areas around Derr and around Ibrim had prospered to some degree despite, or perhaps in part because of, the foreign garrisons sent by the Ottomans to Egyptian Nubia, the southernmost outpost of their empire. Not only Kurds and Hungarians, but also mercenary soldiers from many distant regions of the Oriental and Occidental Turkish world, came to Nubia, where they perished, departed, or intermarried with the local population and settled there. The mixed origins of these Nubians' forebears are still reflected in such local family names as Magari and Kurdi. During this long and obscure period of foreign intrusions into the southern region of Egyptian Nubia, a succession of hereditary Muslim overlords, entitled Kāshifs, became established. These men, absorbed into the Nubian community, had brought with them the education and literacy of the wider Islamic congregation. Under their supervision, mosques and Quranic schools were built, which served to indicate to the world at large that here indeed was a congrega-

[3] James August St. John, *Egypt and Mohammed Ali, or Travels in the Valley of the Nile*, I, 380–381.
[4] Ibid., pp. 386–387.
[5] Ibid., p. 366.
[6] Ibid., p. 438.

tion of Muslims—a community thereby excluded from predatory slave raids.

The Kāshifs of Ottoman times were replaced by Mohammed Ali with his own administrative officers, also called Kāshifs. Their rule was often tyrannical.[7] Through intermarriage, however, many Fedija Nubians trace descent from these men, as well as from Ottoman Kāshifs, and it is still a source of some prestige. Even after the advent of British colonial administration, Kāshif descendants retained considerable local authority in some Nubian communities.

When, in 1811, Mohammed Ali struck down the Mameluke leaders in Cairo, many Mamelukes fled south and caused much destruction; there is little doubt that they were responsible for some of the desolation reported by St. John. Some Mamelukes, upon reaching Nubia, attempted to challenge the position of the Kāshifs appointed by Mohammed Ali and establish themselves at Qasr Ibrim among the Fedija Nubians. These last invaders of Nubia failed to secure their position, were driven from Egyptian Nubia, and were finally captured and returned to Lower Egypt.

Between 1880 and 1900, Great Britain assumed control in Egypt and the Sudan and finally ended the slave trade along the Nile. Kāshif rule also was ended. For the first time, the Nubians were left free to attend to their own affairs without the interference of a local aristocracy and without fear of slave raids. According to one Nubian, "During the period of British authority we were like the man in the middle in bed between two others. Although the man on each side of the bed pulled the blanket back and forth, the man in the middle was never uncovered, and remained warm and secure."

Several points emerge from this brief survey. First,

[7] A tale from Ballana illustrates the high-handed ways of the Kāshifs, even after loss of official recognition: The wife from a rich and powerful Kāshif family used to reserve the right to go through the luggage of Nubian labor migrants who returned to Ballana villages with presents from the city for their families. She took for herself the items that pleased her before distribution to the family could occur. This is said to have happened to the grandparents of older Nubians near the turn of this century.

it seems improbable that Nubia ever was a highly integrated or complex society. The topography of the region and its meager resources generally limited such development. Only the richest communities could support a stratified society; the number of such communities fluctuated with the prosperity of the region, and they were probably not larger than small market towns. Throughout history, Nubia remained primarily a long, narrow, and irregularly spaced succession of villages along the Nile; except in Dongola, no other more cohesive form of settlement was possible. Christian and Muslim hierarchies could thus rise and fall, and their effect on the majority of Nubian settlements was largely absorbed by the stronger and more persistent patterns of village life.

Invasion and colonization in Nubia resulted in intermarriage and assimilation. The invaders were always men, and the Nubian women thus remained a stable and permanent force in the society, passing on their traditions to their children. Finally, over many centuries, slavery touched the lives of Nubians, though this experience varied within the area. The major effects of slavery on Nubian society were twofold. At various times, it created dangerous insecurity in most communities and prevented them from developing their own resources. Second, slavery prejudicially affected social attitudes toward Nubians in Egypt and elsewhere in the Middle East. Obviously, however, the Nubians of today are not the descendants of slaves; those unfortunate people who were victims of the slave trade were, as we have said, lost to their own communities forever.

Entry into the modern world in the nineteenth century as Muslims ended the long period when Nubians were often at the mercy of more powerful neighbors. As Muslims, they had the freedom to develop their own villages again and were permitted to travel to the cities of the Middle East, as free men, to seek employment. The period of ignorance in Nubia was at an end, the Nubians' status as members of the Islamic community assured. This was a time of great development, a golden age of Nubian culture.

3. Nubian Origins

The relationship of the present Nubians to the ancient populations of Egypt and Sudan and to the Nubian kingdoms of Kush has yet to be fully established by archaeologists and historians. However, we do know that contemporary Nubians are a mixture of many peoples. The African, Arabic, and Mediterranean contributions to the population may be surmised from the Nubians' appearance and have been recently demonstrated in studies of blood types. Some tentative explanations of how this process occurred may be inferred from the more recent history related in Chapter 2. Here we are concerned with linguistic and geographic evidence, to help identify the major groupings within the Nubian people before resettlement. Language distribution is also relevant in examining relations between the Nubians and their neighbors, particularly those of Upper Egypt.

Upper Egypt, home of the Sa°īdī peoples, conventionally is defined as the area from Asyūt south to Aswan. On the outskirts of Aswan, the Nubian villages began and extended south along the Nile past the Egyptian Sudanese border to Khartoum. If, however, we accept the Nubian view of the location of their people, Nubians are also to be found north of Aswan town, in the rich agricultural areas around

Esna, Edfu, Daraw, and Kom Ombo. The inhabitants of many villages in the region look Nubian, being somewhat darker than other Egyptians. Members of an old Upper Egyptian tribal grouping, the Ga°afra, these people are generally considered to be Sa°īdīs like their neighbors, and it would be difficult to make a clear-cut separation between the various groups in the area. However, many Ga°afra believe they are related to the Nubians, a belief reciprocated by the Nubians themselves.

The Fedija, Nubians of the South, have described the Ga°afra people as "Arab Egyptianized" Nubians with whom they feel at home and share similar attitudes and life styles, even though they no longer share a common language. The Ga°afra apparently feel somewhat the same way, for, during the years of the British Mandate, many young men from these villages reportedly chose to serve not in the regular divisions of the Egyptian army but in the Hagana, the Sudanese border unit, which contained a large percentage of Nubians.

Aside from the possibly related Ga°afra, few Nubians lived north of the Aswan Dam until their total resettlement near Kom Ombo in 1963. However, some villages had been relocated north of Aswan in the early part of the twentieth century, after they had been displaced by the raising of the earlier dam. The first principal all-Nubian villages, before final resettlement, were found south of the Esna–Kom Ombo region, across the old dam and the First Cataract. These were Kenuzi settlements. The existence here of the Kenuz, occupying approximately one-third of Egyptian Nubia south of Aswan, continues to be a major puzzle for the student of Nubian history. The Kenuz speak a Nubian language that is understood and shared by the people of Dongola, in the Sudan, more than a thousand miles to the south. Yet nothing in the oral traditions of the Nubians or in historical accounts tells us when or how the geographic division took place between the ancestors of the two populations. The close similarity of their speech suggests, however, that it occurred not too many centuries ago.

If, as we presume, the Kenuz and the Dongolawī were once one people, who separated from whom? The Dongolawī people are much the larger of the two groups and lived in the most fertile and ample region of the Upper Nile, whereas the Kenuz in Egyptian Nubia are a small minority of approximately fifty thousand persons. The best evidence, however, that the Kenuz were immigrants from Dongola is probably linguistic, in that there is historical evidence of a language boundary at the southern border of Dongola (where it is today) as early as the late tenth century, whereas Old Nubian documents record no dialect boundary in Egyptian Nubia at that time.[1] Nubians have suggested that perhaps the Kenuz were originally a trade colony, sent by a Dongolawī kingdom to look after trade and shipment at the First Cataract at Aswan, the old port city that marked the boundary on the Nile between Egypt and the ancient Christian kingdoms of Nubia.

In Pharaonic times Aswan produced, not grain, but granite for sculptures; but it was also a rich and important entrepôt and border station and continued to be so in medieval times, long after the Muslim conquest of Egypt in the seventh century. The region between Dongola and Aswan was occupied by several often independent and mutually antagonistic political entities during much of the Christian era. Thus, it seems plausible that, for both commercial and political reasons, groups of Dongolawī may have clustered under the protection of the Egyptian

[1] William Y. Adams, personal communication.

border station at Aswan, their business being to facilitate shipments of goods between Egypt and Dongola. Camel caravans, assembled south of the First Cataract, could avoid contact with the ancestors of the Fedija Nubians, immediately south of the Kenuz, by traveling overland. This transport history might explain the Kenuzi domination of most of the commerce that (until recently) took place between Aswan, the Kenuzi villages, and the Fedija Nubian villages all the way to Wadi Halfa.

Until half a century ago the large commercial sailboats plying the Nile were almost all owned by Kenuz, and up to the time of resettlement, Kenuzi merchant boatmen regularly traveled up and down the river, peddling their wares in the villages of Fedija Nubians, far from their own homes. Kenuz often seek employment on Egyptian and foreign ships; in fact, some Kenuzi men spend a lifetime in maritime service abroad. The Kenuzi reputation as travelers and tradesmen thus would seem to support the "trade colony" theory of their background.

To see the Kenuz as being of recent, intrusive origin, separating the historic Fedija people from the Gaᶜafra and the rest of the older Saᶜīdī population of Upper Egypt, also helps us to understand the existence of the cultural line between Nubia and Egypt, which has been conventionally drawn at Aswan. Over many generations a grey zone probably existed between the two historic groups, a zone neither totally Saᶜīdī nor totally Fedija, created by frequent social contacts and by intermarriage. The districts north of Aswan town, mentioned above, comprised this zone, a region from which the tough, handsome Egyptian Saᶜīdī has emerged, a mingling of Egyptian, Nubian, and Arabian stock over the last thousand years.

The coming of the Kenuz, a people without historic ties to the other inhabitants, may have created the first sharp division at Aswan, effectively blocking contacts between the older settlers, north and south. Agricultural resources were always very marginal along this stretch of river near the First Cataract and could support in the best of times only a relatively small population. Possibly, the Dongolawī ancestors of the present Kenuzi people, dependent primarily on trade rather than agriculture, had become numerically and linguistically predominant by the time the Beni Kanz came from the desert and overran the area in the eleventh century.

This hypothesis is further strengthened by the somewhat parallel existence of another intrusive population farther south, the small enclave of Arabic-speaking "Nubians" found between the Kenuz and the Fedija, in the Wadi el-Arab region. Many of the men in this intermediate area were descended from members of the Allaqat tribe, which originated in the Nejd of northern Arabia. These Nubians still consider themselves Allaqat and have occasional contacts with the tribe. Their genealogies reveal marriages with both Kenuz and, to a lesser extent, Fedija, but the language has remained exclusively Arabic for most of the men and women in the region. Until very recently these people did not call themselves Nubians at all, and they are now so identified in a political-territorial rather than an ethnic-linguistic sense.

These Arabs explain their presence in Nubia by recalling that they (too) were traders. Situated at a strategic point, where the Nile bent sharply for a brief span, thus making river travel slow and difficult against prevailing winds, the Arabs were able to offer merchants faster and less expensive travel overland. During the days of Kāshif rule in Nubia, from the early seventeenth until the nineteenth century, the ancestors of the present Arab enclave transshipped goods by camel caravan overland from Wadi el-Arab to the towns of the Sudan. Beyond Wadi Halfa, the Second and Dal cataracts made the Nile unnavigable for long stretches; presumably, this natural barrier, combined with the presence of alien forces in the region, made further river shipment impractical.

Thus, by the fifteenth century, when Moslem Arab power had largely, but not entirely, gained ascendancy over Christian Nubia, a Moslem Arab outpost in Egyptian Nubia linked trade partners and kinsmen in Moslem Arab regions of the Sudan by caravan routes. In just this way the Christian ancestors of the Kenuz may have been linked to Christian Dongola, also bridging an alien population in an earlier era.

Beyond the Arab enclave, south of Wadi el-Arab, lay the first villages of the Fedija Nubians.[2] The term *Fedija* raises problems; historically, these people used no term of self-reference other than *Nubi*. *Fedija* is in fact a Kenuzi word that means fellah (peasant), a term that has less than complimentary connotations. The historic relations between these

two groups have not been particularly warm, and the fact that the Fedija have begun to refer to themselves by this term no doubt reflects the several generations of peaceful contact that have passed between the two groups.

Contact between the Fedija Nubians and the Mahas and Sukkot groups farther south was inhibited by the rapids and barren cliffs of the Batn el-Haggar, a thinly populated region that extends from the Second Cataract south of Wadi Halfa to the Dal Cataract. The Fedija share their language with Mahas and Sukkot Nubians, and the house types and other readily observable aspects of their culture are similar. After the Dal Cataract the Nile Valley south to the Third Cataract (the Abri-Delgo Reach) became fertile and supported many large villages of Mahasi-speaking Nubians on both sides of the Nile.

The linguistic boundary between the Mahas-Sukkot peoples and the Dongolawī occurs a few kilometers south of the Third Cataract of the Nile. However, the Third Cataract was neither a great natural obstacle nor an important historical or political boundary and therefore does not explain this linguistic division.

Dongola, with its broad fertile shorelands and islands of rich soil, south of the Third Cataract, is still occupied by people who to some degree identify with the heritage of the ancient kingdom that flourished there, in the cities of Kerma and Old Dongola.

Dongola was beyond the scope of our study of Egyptian Nubia. However, according to one authority, the people of this region "are really Nubian only in speech (which is rapidly disappearing); in all other respects they are as thoroughly Arabized as their cousins, the Shaiqiya and Jaᶜaliyin, and they generally deny a Nubian identity. . . . On the other hand, the Mahasi retain, at least up to now, a definite sense of their special identity and history. Consequently, I would say that the Mahasi of the Abri-Delgo Reach (i.e., those that were not displaced by the Aswan Dam), rather than the Danagla [Dongolawī], represent the probable last refuge of distinctly Nubian culture and traditions."[3]

[2] Elsewhere the term *Mahas* has been used to refer to the Fedija and their language, but Mahas also refers to a Sudanese Nubian group immediately south. The two groups are closely related, but to avoid confusion I utilize only *Fedija* throughout this book.

[3] William Y. Adams, personal communication.

With linguistic divisions and a long history of shifting political boundaries and alliances, how appropriate is it to speak of an autochthonous "Nubian" people? Anthropologist William Y. Adams, who has made the culture history of Nubia an object of extensive archaeological research, has provided an authoritative observation in this regard. "There is very little doubt that until three or four centuries ago (i.e., until the Arabization of the Shaiqiya, Jaᶜaliyin, etc.) Nubians formed a solid linguistic and cultural bloc extending along the Nile from Aswan in the north at least to the junction of the Niles, and probably to Sennar, in the south, and perhaps westward into Kordofan and Darfur as well. How long they may have been in this habitat is uncertain, but I think it was certainly long enough to qualify them as 'autochthonous.' "[4]

The questions as to how long the people we call Nubian have lived in this region, where they may have come from originally, and their possible relationship with the ancient civilizations of Kush,

which once occupied much of Nubia, must await the results of recent (and future) research. The forthcoming study of Nubian history by William Y. Adams will undoubtedly add much to our understanding of these problems.

Use of the term *Nubian* as a self-referent has only become general among the Egyptian Nubians in recent years; a sense of identity has developed as the construction of the High Dam has made Nubians the object of national attention and has presented them with a crisis of overriding importance. At the same time, the construction of the High Dam has permanently divided the Nubians of Egypt from those of Sudan through resettlement. The Nubians of Egypt are no longer a Nilotic people, and the patterns of life developed along the river must now be adjusted to a radically different environment in much closer association with the peoples of Upper Egypt. Before discussing this problem of adjustment, we need to look at the traditional circumstances of Egyptian Nubians in what they refer to as their "golden age," those decades just prior to resettlement.

4 Ibid.

4. The Nubian Polity

Nubians speak of their native land as *balad el-aman*, a land of safety and security, a place where people and property were secure and where one could live in peace. To those of us who, as outsiders, have lived in Nubia, the claims as to the blessed quality of life do not seem exaggerated. One cannot associate violence with this land and people. Nor were the more subtle patterns of factionalism and hostility so evident here as they sometimes are in village life elsewhere. This fundamental impression of the nonviolent, peaceful quality of Nubian life can only be explained or made plausible if we understand what I have chosen to call the Nubian polity. Polity, in this sense, involves economy and ecology, as well as the kinship organization, and the values and attitudes associated with these basic conditions of everyday life.

Social organization in the traditional Nubian village was simple, in the sense that no special officers existed who made executive decisions or judged conflicts. The same patterns of association between individuals that sufficed to carry on the work of cultivation managed to resolve the conflicts that are everywhere a part of human relationships. Whatever the political institutions of the past may have been during the Christian period, for instance, or

during the days of Turkish Kāshif rule, these were largely forgotten by the time of our studies. Until the building of the High Dam and the consequent resettlement, Nubians, though technically subject to the administrative authority of Cairo, remained largely free of outside interference. Many villagers we visited by sailboat and donkey could not remember when a stranger had last approached their shores. The occasional administrators from the central ministries in Cairo confined their visits largely to the *omda*, the locally selected, but government-appointed Nubian who acted as liaison between the villages of his district and the outside world. The Nubian villages, poor in resources, and of slight political significance, had little interest for the national government. Only after the Nasser revolution of 1952 did a more benevolent form of interference begin to appear in the form of schools, subsidized staple foods, fuel, and occasional medical services. But these comparatively recent developments had still not touched the lives of all the villages prior to resettlement.

Although the Nubian villages were tied to cities hundreds of miles away through a pattern of labor migrancy we shall discuss later, in terms of their everyday life they were isolated far beyond the degree characteristic of many peasant communities, where trips to the city market regularly break the seasonal routine. The desolate environment behind the villages tied the people more closely to the edge of the Nile than most peasants are tied to their communities. Movement from village to village was difficult; boat travel was slow where it existed at all, and moving along the Nile by donkey from one village to the next took time and effort. Cities of any size were hundreds of miles away—so that until this century little contact existed between Nubian villagers and the outside world.

When peaceful conditions permitted the Nubians to live in their villages and cultivate with some security, efforts were made to cultivate all of the very limited arable land. Irrigation was necessary, and in some areas local conditions made practicable the construction of water wheels (*eskalay*), an invention introduced in Roman times, which, at that time, significantly increased cultivation. Where shore conditions or the paucity of exposed alluvium did not justify the expense of water-wheel construction, a second device, the *keeyay*, or water-bucket lift, was used, although the *keeyay* conveyed only a small fraction of the water that an *eskalay* could handle. Since the land irrigated by either device was likely to be strictly limited, it is not surprising that the word *eskalay* means not only water wheel but also the land cultivated by means of this mechanism.

In the Fedija area, where water wheels persisted until the resettlement of 1963, construction of an *eskalay* required a concentration of wealth often beyond the means of those owning the adjacent land.[1] The wooden piles that had to be driven into the muddy shore of the Nile, the complex wheels that dipped an endless chain of clay buckets into the water, the platform on which a pair of cows turned the mechanism, and the hollow logs that carried the water to the farm land were all individually valued, different families taking responsibility for the construction of these expensive parts. The total cost was more than a single household might accumulate in a lifetime.

The Fedija Nubians point to the great expense of

[1] For more detailed information about the *eskalay* and its operation, see Abdel Hamid El-Zein, "Socio-economic implications of the water wheel in Adendan, Nubia," in *Contemporary Egyptian Nubia*, ed. Robert A. Fernea, II, 298–322; and "Water and wheel in a Nubian village," M.A. thesis, American University in Cairo.

the *eskalay* to explain the mixture of families in some villages. Any man who could share the investment necessary to build a water wheel acquired a right to a share of the produce of the *eskalay*; this in turn might encourage him to settle a son near the *eskalay* through marriage with a principal landowner, for a Nubian bride customarily brought with her a certain amount of land, which the bridegroom added to his own inheritance as the basic resource for the new family. The Nubians of Ballana remember that the Kāshif often obliged Nubians to give them a daughter in marriage in exchange for an interest in an *eskalay*.

Water wheels were land-water-machine complexes instituted by means of shared investments. The principal means of avoiding excessive division of the complex through inheritance was marriage. Marriage linked the co-owners of the wheel and the land, and subsequently their offspring; since Nubians prefer marriage between relatives, especially paternal cousins, these unions frequently rewove the strands of kinship between descendants and co-owners. As married couples, the intermarrying cousins in effect added together the same inherited interests that their fathers, as brothers, had divided.

Nor was this pattern of kinship networks and shared economic interests limited to the *eskalay*. Palm trees were another important example of the same phenomenon. The initial ownership of a palm tree was usually based on a three-way partnership between a landowner, the owner of the palm shoot, and the person (usually a woman) who watered the shoot constantly over the many months before it got its growth and could draw sufficient moisture through its own roots. As a result of these investments of labor, real estate, and "capital," the ownership of the palm tree was divided three ways, but, as the shares were subsequently divided between heirs or given to children as wedding gifts, the rights to the fruit of the tree became widely diffused and each Nubian was likely to be involved in many such minicorporate marriage and descent networks, no one with exactly the same composition as the next. At the time of the date harvest one saw groups sitting under the trees, the fruit from each tree being divided and subdivided into little piles of dates, usually under the general direction of the old women who best remembered the complicated rights of ownership involved.

Hundreds of people from up and down the Nile would come by sailboat to attend the *moulids*, or saint's day celebrations held each year in the northern Kenuzi villages.

Mothers and daughters walked in procession to the shrine of the saint during the *moulid*.

Cows, also, were corporately owned and were an essential source of power in the traditional Nubian economy, being the only creatures used to turn the heavy water wheels. Without these animals, the wheels stood idle and the fields untilled. Yet, cows, subject to death and sickness, were a rapidly depreciating investment, somewhat redeemed by the possibility of calving. Following the general pattern of shared resource ownership, most farmers had interests in several cows, a "leg," or one quarter, of the cow being a common share. The person who sheltered and fed the cow when it was not working was entitled to its milk and calves as compensation (though these arrangements varied); each of the other co-owners had to feed and water the cow during the twelve-hour shift that the animal worked on their *eskalay*. Each *eskalay* had a piece of land set aside for raising feed for the cows when they worked a shift at the wheel, thus eliminating arguments over dividing responsibility for feed among the various owners of the *eskalay*.

Buying shares in a cow was a relatively high yielding if somewhat risky investment for the Nubian with extra cash. He could buy cow or calf shares up for sale, leave the animals in the stables of the other owners, and collect rent on their use (a share of the crop being irrigated), since he then owned more rights to cow labor than he needed himself. A study of cow ownership by Abdul Hamid El Zein reveals a very complex stock-market-like situation with price fluctuations, marginal buying, and monopolistic potentials. Cows sometimes became a source of social discord, and thus it was probably well for the peace of the Nubian society that *eskalay* and palm shares, after the initial investment, were never sold or traded like cow shares, but only inherited or bestowed upon the young as gifts.

The significance of the system of shared ownership goes well beyond economic considerations. An annual trip to a neighboring village to collect a few handfuls of dates clearly had more social importance in terms of maintaining relationships with the collateral branches of the family than in terms of the actual material value involved. "We know the family is still together," said one Fedija Nubian, "when it gathers to divide the produce from land or date trees owned by our great-great-grandfathers. When the shareholders say 'I don't care; help yourself,' then we know the big family is breaking up."

In the case of the *eskalay*, one or two men usually cultivated the land as part owners as well as sharecroppers for the frequently numerous other shareholders. Many of the shareholders might be away working in the cities of Egypt or the Sudan, having relinquished their rights to the produce of the *eskalay* for years. The important consideration was that the absent villager owned shares that were remembered and that could be activated should he or other members of his immediate family return for a visit or settle again in the village. The basic resources of Nubia not only served to sustain the families that actively utilized them, but also helped to maintain social ties with the large percentage of residents who lived and worked elsewhere. In such ingenious fashion the villages and extended families of Nubia managed to hold the loyalties of many more individuals than the strictly limited resources could support.

Without recognized rights to land and palm trees, the individual migrant's tie to the village had no substance; claiming or retaining rights to a share of the village produce was tantamount to public recognition of membership in a descent group represented in the village. If one has recognized kinship in a Nubian community, then one must by the same token have some claim to the community's resources. Cow shares are sold and bought, but other property rights become available only as gifts at marriage or through inheritance and, of course, can only be disposed of in the same manner.

In peasant villages and urban settings throughout the world, the inheritance of property is both the greatest threat and the greatest source of strength to bonds of kinship. How many families are irrevocably divided because of quarrels over inheritance? How many claim the loyalty of their members because of a persistent interest in family property? I have suggested that Nubian society would be threatened with total extinction if its economic resources were not used because of disputes over property ownership; this theory still does not explain why such disputes do not generally occur. The reasons for such an unusually peaceful state of affairs lie partly in urban attitudes and values and partly in the Nubian kinship system.

The Kenuzi and Fedija Nubians differ significantly in their systems of kinship, for the influence of the Beni Kanz Arabs on the natives of what is now the Kenuzi region transformed that society into a segmentary tribal organization not unlike that of Arab tribes found elsewhere in the Middle East.[2] Tribal groups were distributed over a number of villages, divided into maximum lineages, subdivided into secondary lineages, and finally separated into individual families—all reckoned on the basis of descent from a common ancestor. In the past the tribal system of the Kenuz may have been closely linked to property rights, but our evidence for this is limited. At the time of the Nubian Ethnological Survey, much of the land in the Kenuzi region had disappeared under the waters backed up by the dams constructed before the High Dam at Aswan. Neither palm trees nor *eskalays* existed in the Kenuzi village at the time of our studies. Only in the saints' shrines that dotted the area did the tribe actively share a common interest with common responsibilities at certain specific times of the year during the *moulid* celebrations (these will be discussed in more detail subsequently).

The Fedija Nubians, on the other hand, were still able to cultivate much of their ancestral land in the southernmost districts of Ballana and Adendan and were generally better off than their Kenuzi neighbors to the north. As late as 1962, the large stands of date palms in the Ballana, Adendan, and Abu Simbel districts were still an important source of income for the villages. Thus, it was possible, at the time of the survey, to see something of the way in which kinship organization controlled the peaceful and sustained exploitation of the meager natural resources.

The Fedija refer to all units of family membership as *nog(s)*.[3] A man's first *nog* is his household, the group of people for whom he is economically and socially responsible, including his wife, or wives, and children, as well as any other relatives who live in his house and are dependent on him for support. (Few Nubians have more than one wife, but those who do feel it is desirable to support the wives in different houses—this is the only situation in which the man's first *nog* will encompass more

than one household.) In other contexts, all of a man's dependents may be referred to as his *nog*. Only with marriage does one acquire the *nog*, or responsibility of an adult; the *nog* is the primary group that pays a man respect and is obedient to him.

The best definition of the second *nog* is also a function of how it operates; the second *nog* is comprised of those relatives with whom one still divides the products of land and trees, no matter how small the shares may have become. Therefore, most men have two, largely overlapping *nogs*: the *nog* of one's father, wherein most of the household property is shared, and the *nog* of one's mother. The matrilineal *nog* is often very close in composition to the patrilineal *nog*, since, by preference, many marriages are between men and women who share patrilineal ancestors. Yet, a mother is likely to have received some shares of property from a relative who did not provide property for her husband, and the children will be involved with both sets of people. Where a man has made an exogamous marriage, the mother's *nog* will, of course, involve her children with another largely different set of people.

The bilateral *nogs* are not only of economic importance to the child. "Mother's relatives" remain a separate and important category even when mother and father are paternal cousins. As one Nubian explained it, "My mother's relatives were those men [and women] whom I met while they were in the house with her; my father's [male] relatives were men I met outside with him." Although in Nubian society social segregation of males and females is not nearly so rigorously practiced as in many traditional Arab settings, men do not ordinarily venture into the private quarters of a house unless they are the brothers, fathers, or husbands of the women of the house, or are kinsmen who, through family tradition, have long been intimates of the household. Thus, even in this society of endogamous marriages, the child's world is divided into two sets of relatives: the indulgent, loving group around the mother with whom one can behave with great informality, and the group surrounding the father—those who represent the family in society, who care for its honor, and who must be accorded respect lest a son blacken the reputation of his own kinsmen by appearing not to care about his father's dignity.

The child owes less to the matrilineal *nog* and,

---

[2] Since this manuscript was written, Dr. Charles Callender has published with Fadwa el Guindi *Life crisis rituals among the Kenuz*, which should be consulted for further information about the Kenuz.

[3] I am indebted to Bahiga Haikal El Ghamry, who first brought the importance of the *nog* to my attention.

materially, is likely to receive less. Yet, many Nubians mention being taken by their mothers some distance from the home village to attend a division of dates among the mother's relatives. Many Fedija men can recite the maternal lineage of their mother almost as readily as that of their father, going back seven or eight generations, and a number of Nubian men carry the mother's rather than the father's name as their own second name. For example, instead of being called Abdulla *Hassan*, the name of his father, a man might be called Abdulla *Fatooma*, the latter being his mother's name. Abdulla Fatooma would not officially be the man's name, but it would be the name by which he was called.

In a number of ways, the Nubian kinship organization resembles American kin systems more than that of most Arabs, who much more exclusively emphasize patrilineal descent and relationship. (I, for example, am "Alta's boy" in some situations and "George's boy" in others.) However, as the child moves to the most inclusive and public kinship group to which he belongs, the emphasis on paternal descent is reasserted. The largest *nog* includes a large number of smaller *nogs* spread over a number of villages and districts and is defined as these men (and their household *nogs*) who bear the same family name.

While the members of the largest *nog* presumably share a common paternal ancestor, though he may be ten or twelve generations in the past, the largest *nog* does not usually carry the name of that ancestor, as is characteristic among the Arabs. Rather, the name of the *nog* often refers to some quality or outstanding event in the experience of the group. One important *nog* of this largest type is the Fagirob, who are found in several districts and many villages near the Sudanese-Egyptian border. The Fagirob trace their ancestry eleven generations back to a man named Sharif, but the group's name (Fagir, i.e., Fakir) came into use because, it is said, the men of this group at one time were religious teachers of the Sufi persuasion; many Fagirob still claim a particular interest in religion. This use of an adjectively derived name, rather than a specific ancestor's name, gives the system considerable flexibility. Family identity may be maintained among the widest possible group of people, not only those directly descended from the common ancestor, and permits movement into the group as well as move-

ment out of the group through migration and loss of contact. For example, descendants of a man married to a Fagirob woman might eventually call themselves Fagirob, particularly if the property they inherited was from the mother's people.

A man's largest *nog* is thus not strictly divided into lineages, as in Arab tribes, but rather consists of smaller *nogs* composed of men who share property. The *nogs* are overlapping, in the sense that a man may own shares in several different groups, not all of which are his closest kinsmen. This feature is very important, for, unlike the Arab tribe, the Nubian *nog* does not split easily into opposing segments of kinsmen.

While the Fedija Nubians know of the Arab feud, they have no memory of such a custom, and indeed, given the nature of their *nogs*, it is difficult to see how the feud could have developed; feuds usually require sharp definitions between "us" and "them," which hardly seem possible in the flexible Nubian kinship system we have described. To pin on the Fedija kinship system the conventional classificatory terms used by anthropologists (which largely depend on the way in which descent is reckoned) is to unduly formalize the system.

Because more individuals have rights to shares of village harvests than could possibly subsist from them if all the rights were exercised, and because many individuals must find their living in the cities and help support their dependents in the villages, the precise composition of any given *nog* is impossible to predict, whether it be a household *nog*, where one survey revealed twenty different combinations of relatives living under the same roof, or the larger *nog* composed of all people sharing the same family name. A Nubian village is not only a place where a minority of men can live and work as farmers, cultivating their own and other's shares of land; it is also a place to which the widow returns from Cairo to find a home with a brother, a place to which a migrant returns temporarily to marry or to rest between city jobs, and particularly a place where women and children stay with the head of their household *nog* when no room can be found in the city. To reiterate, all the villagers, both absent and present, have rights of their own in their villages that have been relinquished to others in their absence but that, if contacts have been maintained with their kinsmen, may be resumed once more when and if they return to their ancestral homes. The demographic facts of a high birth rate and limited resources must also be kept in mind if one is to understand the relationship between the ecology, the economy, and the kinship organization of Nubia. Kinship bears a close relationship to the Nubian polity and particularly to the remarkable absence of violence and serious quarrels found in Nubian communities.

With other peoples of the Middle East, Nubians share a strong sense of responsibility for helping others resolve their differences. Strangers inevitably crowd around a street quarrel, add their voices to the argument, comment on the merits of both sides, separate the principals if violence seems imminent, and offer suggestions to resolve the difficulty. Whether within the family or on the street, the Middle Eastern ethic is the exact opposite of the Western practice of "staying out of other people's business." When a non-Arabic-speaking American sees a group of people gathered on a street surrounding two men on the point of serious fighting, the Westerner fears a street brawl and rushes away; if he could understand what is being said in the crowd he would realize that an ad hoc process of conflict resolution is taking place and the protagonists are being offered honorable ways of withdrawing from the contest.

When quarrels occur among relatives, however, the case is somewhat different. Such quarrels are regarded by most Middle Easterners, and particularly Nubians, as extremely dangerous. Every effort must be expended to resolve these situations within the family and to do so as quickly as possible. Why? Quarrels weaken and divide the only group of people on whom an individual can depend, one's own relatives. Factionalism divides kin groups, reduces the number of individuals involved in mutual assistance, and can result in leaving one alone and exposed to the hostility of strangers, too weak to maintain a position in the economy and the society. Until the last few decades, the idea of turning one's back on kith and kin to find independently a job, or a wife, or a residence was quite alien to Middle Eastern society.

Obviously, the Nubians' sharing of resources could be a prime source of conflict as well as an integrative force. Relatives of several household *nogs* (who together constituted the intermediate *nog* sharing kinship and rights to *eskalays* and palm trees) must agree on the ways in which these resources are to be utilized, on the individuals who are to benefit, to subsist from the resources, and on who is to retain only residual rights to them. How did the Nubians decide who should stay in the village and farm and who should immigrate to the city, who should remain in the city and who should return home? The question is partly answered in our forthcoming discussion of Nubian marriage, but it seems still a logical source of contention, just as the many divisions of crops that each harvest brings forth might be the subject of serious quarrel; how is it that these divisions are regarded as celebrations of family unity rather than sources of disagreement?

The real danger of quarrels over harvests and resource usage lies, of course, in the possibility that the *eskalays* might fall into disuse. But many men, extended networks of kinsmen, have sentimental and material interests in the *eskalay* or the palm trees. The resources are the symbol of the kin's unity and their tie with grandfathers long dead, as well as the source of their daily bread. Therefore, an ample number of kinsmen would be linked to both sides of a dispute among relatives, ready to mediate differences and reconcile antagonists. No matter what the exact relationship between the disputants might be, intermediaries, the *wasta*, or "go-betweens" found in many Arab communities, can and do come forward to carry messages back and forth between disagreeing groups to find a compromise and, if necessary, to help shame the principals into reconciling their differences.

The fundamental Nubian conviction that each adult man or woman has a basic responsibility to intercede in quarrels between those kinsmen and neighbors with whom one shares some identity of interests is well illustrated by a Nubian anecdote of apparently recent origin, a combination of an old story and a new one.

The old story concerns two men who were constantly quarreling over the division of water provided by an *eskalay* they shared. To irrigate both pieces of land that the two men owned, the water had to be channeled first into one ditch and then into another. One of the men was always accusing the other of taking more than his share of water until their uncle overheard the two men arguing. The uncle thought about the situation briefly and then walked away, only to return in a moment with a stone, which he placed in the middle of the canal, thus effectively dividing the water into two streams and putting an end to the source of contention.

The new variation of the story involves the nationalization of the Suez Canal in 1956. During the brief military conflict between the British and the Egyptians, several Nubians hurried back and forth between fields and villages to listen to the latest news on a shortwave battery radio. Along the path over which the men hurried, an old man sat under a palm tree. He would struggle to his feet to ask what was happening, only to have the men pass by quickly in the opposite direction. Finally, in frustration and annoyance, he grabbed one of the younger men as he rushed by and demanded to know what the commotion was about. "Grandfather," the young man said, "the British and the Egyptians are fighting over the Suez Canal!" The old man reflected on this for a moment and then asked, "What's the matter with them? Couldn't they find anyone to put a stone in the middle?"

Putting a stone in the middle is a political art at which the Nubians are extremely skilled and that they take very seriously. Most frequently, quarrels between kinsmen are resolved quickly by a third, usually older relative. If more kinsmen become involved in the dispute, or if the quarrel concerns a serious matter not amenable to private diplomacy, the Fedija Nubians may call a family council of the larger, property-sharing *nog*. Then all the resident kinsmen gather—not only men, but women and children as well. An elder kinsman presides over the council, one who has come to be accepted as a spokesman for this extended group of kinsmen, the intermediate *nog* referred to commonly, for example, as "Hamza's people."

The leader of "Hamza's people" is expected to hear both sides of the argument, to let all parties present their cases, and, finally, to make a judgment that he senses will receive support from the majority of third parties present. One well-known Fedija leader commonly settled matters by relying on the fact that, in most quarrels between men, one man was very likely to be somewhat older than the other. In this case, he would make the younger man kiss the elder person's head, asking his forgiveness because he had not respected a person older than himself. Then the leader would oblige the older man to embrace the younger in front of the family gathering, asking his forgiveness for having tempted the youth into showing disrespect to his elders by quarreling with him!

Conflict resolution takes a more serious tone in violent offenses, such as physical injury, rape, or murder. The news of such offenses is kept from women and children, the matter is not discussed publicly, and only the men of the *nog* gather to hear the case. The sanction in such cases may be social death for the offender, who would then be required to give up all his possessions and property rights and leave the community forever. If the culprit refused, the men of the village would refuse to speak to him until complete social and economic ostracism would oblige the guilty party to leave.

On the other hand, should a defendant take his problem to the police, he would receive the same treatment as the offender! For violence not only threatened the moral standard of the community, but also exposed the village to the peril of outside intervention in community affairs. Crimes would then be punished according to alien laws in ways that could be far more detrimental to the general welfare of the village than the consequences of the original mistake. The greatest protection of the weak is secrecy, a fact known to peasant villagers throughout the world and one that the Nubian has learned well. Egyptian police on duty in Eneiba, the administrative center of Ballana, in the Fedija region, often complained of boredom in their position; aside from minor smuggling, they said, there was no crime in Nubia. Researchers in the area had an identical impression. Yet, if crimes of violence had occurred, no outsiders, in accordance with Nubian standards, would ever have known of them.

No feuds, no fractious disputes over shared resources, no pervasive factionalism in the villages, no violence—even if this picture is not entirely a true one and appears to be so partly because of an outsider's ignorance, it is a fact that this is the Nubian's image of his own society and one in which he takes great pride. Within the closely woven fabric of kinship and economics, ample numbers of peacemakers can be found to resolve every quarrel, and other conditions of Nubian life also complement this situation by reducing possible sources of tension. Migration is one such condition.

By the middle of the twentieth century almost

every Nubian male had spent part of his adult life working in an Egyptian or a Sudanese city, and in recent years wives accompanied them in increasing numbers. Even though a migrant in the city was not hidden from his other migrant relatives, the urban setting unquestionably provided greater privacy of action and freedom from social constraint than did the village in Nubia. The village was the conservative end of this bipolar world, a place to be revered in the conversations of the migrant, to be honored and idealized—but hardly the place for a young man who wished to explore the pleasures of alcohol and women and to publicly carouse occasionally with age mates. Migration was thus an outlet for high-spirited and adventurous youth, and more than one dignified elder, who appeared the soul of respectability in his village retirement, was whispered to have been quite a rake in Cairo in the old days. The most discontented villagers were the young male schoolteachers, who, although scarcely libertine themselves, felt rebuffed and constrained by the excessive conservatism of their natal community. In a number of villages, for instance, the older men, allying themselves with younger religious conservatives, periodically attempted to forbid dancing at weddings, a pleasure the younger people much enjoyed. Such discrepancies in attitude between young and old were as serious a source of tension in Nubia as in any other small community. For Nubian villages, like many other Middle Eastern communities, were places where formality, respect, and constraint characterized the relations between generations. Nearly all informal, voluntary socializing and recreational activity was confined to gatherings of peers.

Kinsmen of one's father's generation were treated with the respect accorded one's parent: no lounging about, smoking, or casual conversation was permitted in their presence; when passing by on a donkey, one should dismount and greet such men. Young married men not working in the city constituted another, very important clique in most communities. Since marriage was the mark of adulthood, this energetic group pushed to play a role as men in their community, sometimes in opposition to their father's peer group. In another category were the young unmarried men and the grandfathers of the community who found themselves in a similar position, one waiting for the days of social importance and the other having passed them, as in the song

the Nubian musician Hamza El Din sings, of the grandfather visiting with his grandson, both ignored by the rest of the family and glad for each other's company.

In societies without more specialized institutions governing the community, the differences in rights and duties based on age are almost as important as those based on sex. The respect for elders drummed into the Nubian child was a strong weapon for the older man who needed to force a reconciliation among his sometimes quarrelsome younger kinsmen. When affairs of common community concern were discussed after the men's Friday prayers at the village mosque, it was generally the younger men who proposed, the older who disposed. But the strains between young and old that this age-grading sometimes exacerbates were greatly relieved by the possibility of labor migration, the alternative between city and country, which many men believed lay open to them.

Another factor contributing to the peacefulness of Nubian life was the definition of misfortune in these communities. Just as in parts of the world where witches are found, human beings in Nubia were sometimes considered the agents of others' misfortunes. The difference was that Nubians believed that these "other people" were not personally to blame for the catastrophes. Rather, they were the unfortunate, but impersonal, possessors of the evil eye. Every village had one or more men, women, or even children known to have the "eye." Animals fell sick, children got fever, men broke their legs, water jars cracked, and house walls collapsed, all as a result of an envious or admiring glance from a person with such an eye. The only protection was to be inconspicuous, to not draw attention to good fortune, and to ward off the evil eye and render it impotent by using blue beads, Quranic inscriptions, or a charm in the form of a hand. (The latter is known throughout the Middle East as the Hand of Fatima, daughter of the Prophet Mohammed.)

The evil eye then, despite its location in a human being, is an impersonal force in Nubia, a much more humane attitude than that projected by the scapegoat theory of the witch. A man with the "eye" cannot help himself; he has "something missing" in his personality or his life that makes him envious of others' good fortune. This is a Nubian explanation, combining a certain psychological perspective with a view of human destiny and fate. Nubian insistence on the impersonal nature of this force, on the principle that the individual possessing the "eye" is not to blame for the consequences of his glances, is very strong. But people with the "eye" are also expected to be careful with it as much as possible. Men, sitting with a person who is known to have the "eye," will sometimes shout suddenly at him when he absentmindedly falls to staring at something or someone, somewhat in the same way as we do when trying to frighten someone out of the hiccups.

The dangers involved in trying to use the "eye" willfully to harm someone are nicely illustrated by the Nubian story of the farmer who quarreled with his neighbor and decided on what he considered a perfect revenge. He brought an old man with the "eye" to the edge of a dune overlooking the field where his neighbor's cows were pastured. "Look, look down there at those fine cows," he said. "Where?" asked the old man, whose sight was failing. "Down there, under that palm tree off by itself on the left," said the vengeful farmer. "My! What fine eyes you have," said the old man with the "eye."

Attempting to use the evil eye to one's advantage inevitably exposes one to its dangers. This is quite different from using others as scapegoats for individual or collective misfortunes. The Nubians may well be fatalists, a term loosely used to describe many Middle Eastern people, but their fatalism does not prevent them from journeying to Cairo for medical treatment when they are sick and seeking scientific ways of treating their sick cows. It does, however, help keep each personal sorrow in a community from becoming the source of rancor and dispute among people who must live together and share the same resources if they are to survive.

I have tried to outline the social and economic features of Nubian life that help maintain the apparently low levels of factionalism and the high levels of accord in the community. These conditions are not, of course, subject to exact measurement and are unquestionably subject to variation in time and space in ways that cannot be fully taken into account here. They also grew out of need. Shared ownership of resources—palm trees, land, cows, and water wheels—was obviously required in Nubia so that the community might survive. Spreading rela-

tionships and kin ties more broadly over all sections of the community, through the series of flexible social units (nogs), kept feuding and quarreling to a minimum. These relationships were also necessary for the community's survival, as was the development of conflict resolution to a fine art.

The threat posed to the survival of the villages by the high levels of migration must also be acknowledged. Many women and children would have been unable to exist without the subsistence increments provided by urban migrants in the form of thousands of dollars' worth of small postal orders delivered every few weeks on the eagerly awaited post boat. In villages where over half the population was female, few women would have had much hope of marriage were not the absent migrant men sufficiently tied to their village and kin to want to return and marry their cousins and neighbors. Once again, the Nubians improvised ways of dealing with the possible loss of the men of the community. The shared resource base and the kinship system have already been mentioned. But, in addition, the importance of the city-to-village tie is expressed in other ways. Many formalities, for instance, are associated both with leave-taking and with arrival. The wife is the first to say good-by to her migrant husband and the last to greet him when he arrives, as he takes leave of every village household before his departure on the Sudanese post boat and greets each house when he returns via the same boat. A man living in Cairo is expected to send telegrams of condolence when a death occurs in the village and to pay a call at the household of his deceased relative or neighbor as soon as he returns to the home village.

Death ceremonies are, in fact, occasions at which attendance is most stringently required. During the three-day mourning period, all the members of the smallest, intermediate, and largest nog visit the home of the bereaved. Sailboats may arrive from districts several miles away, bringing together members of the largest kin group, who may not have seen each other since the last member of the nog died. Women gather inside the house of the bereaved, while the men sit together in temporary structures constructed outside especially for the occasion. Of course, attendance at mourning ceremonies varies with the age and importance of the deceased; young children bring together only kinswomen and the men of the immediate family, while an important elder may require the attendance of hundreds of people and bring dozens of telegrams from all over Sudan and Egypt. Still, whenever a death occurs, women will pass the news on from village to village, dropping whatever they may be doing and flocking to the home of the dead person, often bringing food to help care for the visitors who may be coming from greater distances and spending one or more nights. Once more, the system of *karray* exchanges (to be discussed later) is invoked and utilized. The person who fails to carry out the expected pattern of behavior on such occasions, who does not do for the bereaved family what was done the last time a death occurred in *his* family, will suffer the disapproval of the entire community. A migrant who fails to send condolences is often spoken of as dead himself—indeed, an accurate expression, since neglect of this fundamental social duty is tantamount to a public declaration that the offender is no longer interested in his village or kinsmen, and has parted forever from his Nubian community.

Well over half of every Nubian village lived away in the city; the household economy of most families depended on some support from absent members as well as on the shares of land relinquished in absence. This was one of the most fundamental facts of Nubian life before resettlement, and, lest the peacefulness of village life in Nubia seem to be a romanticized notion, one should remember that a great deal of that life was, in effect, lived hundreds of miles away. Unlike villages elsewhere in the world whose boundaries are finite and who can offer no alternative to the inhabitants, the villages of Nubia were easy to leave and the efforts of the remaining inhabitants were mobilized to retain ties to their absentee members. The basic problem was to see that resources were effectively used at home while the migrants made their way to the city, mindful of their responsibilities and ties to their native land.

One must still give the Nubians great credit for devising careful, nonviolent solutions to the problems of limited resources and of migration, a cultural approach they have also brought to bear on their life in the cities.

5. The Fedija Marriage Ceremony

Nubians, in explaining the nature of their "blessed" society to outsiders, often begin by describing the marriage ceremony. As the various steps of the marriage arrangements unfold, other networks of relationships within the society emerge, expressed somewhat differently than in a formal economic analysis. Drawing heavily on customs of the Fedija area, let us look at Nubia in this way for a moment.

Agreements to marry, according to the Nubians, may be made while the principals are still infants; some women are said to marry off children even before they are born! One day, of course, the bride and groom must themselves agree to such a union, but resistance to a long-standing family decision is difficult. In other cases, a boy may know a girl and wish to marry her but leave the arrangements to his parents, after he has first persuaded them of the wisdom of the decision. But since shareholdings and family relationships are basic considerations underlying all decisions about marriage, in general it is the adults who tend to initiate marriage talks.

The woman in question is also a basic consideration, and problems of shareholdings do not preclude visits by women of the boy's house to the house of the girl's family, particularly if the families do not already know each other well. Not only the girl's appearance, but also her manner and behavior are scrutinized. Nubians particularly appreciate grace and poise in a woman, and the bridegroom's family notes carefully the girl's ability to serve visitors with dignity and without nervousness.

If all goes well, the engagement, *firgar*, is formalized by a visit to the girl's home by the boy's closest relatives. A meal is served and the bride-to-be's father announces the reason for the occasion. The oldest or most respected man present asks God's blessing upon the prospective marriage, following which all the people recite the Fatiha (the first sura, or verse, of the Quran). Often a reciprocal visit to the groom's house by the bride's family takes place, which helps facilitate the many arrangements that must be made before the final ceremony.

For the public announcement of the engagement, the bride's father will slaughter an animal (*gojir*). All members of the villages and the *nogs* of both the bride and the groom are invited, indeed obligated, to partake of the feast. Failing to attend such an occasion is not as serious as neglecting to offer condolences upon a death, but it is a very grave insult, nonetheless. The father of the groom reciprocates with a second feast for the community.

These occasions are made possible by another level of reciprocity that is of fundamental importance in Nubian society. Each household, each adult, is linked to others through favors received and favors owed. The exchanges, *karray*, serve to mobilize the community's resources for private ceremonies. Each woman for whom the bride's or groom's mother has done simple favors will bring some contribution for the feast: her best cups, perhaps, or some tea, sugar, or loaves of bread. Every married woman, it is said, has her own private stores from which she takes contributions on such occasions. Unmarried young girls, who do not yet have household stores at their disposal, will offer services, to fill the *zirs*, or clay jars, with river water, for example. The partners in the exchange are usually members of the same extended *nog*, but similar gestures are expected among neighbors in the village, whatever the exact kinship.

The evening before the wedding itself is the time for *kofferay dibbi*, a party similar to the *layla el-henna*, or night of henna, in Egyptian marriages. The bride and groom are both treated to an elaborate toilette, he with his friends at the river, she in her house, though she may also visit the bank of the river briefly. Henna is applied liberally, and the bride and groom, dressed in their wedding finery and attended by their friends, become the object of entertainment, affection, and teasing. On this evening the couple is considered to be both vulnerable to the evil eye and yet possessed of a special *baraka*, or grace, which sets them somewhat apart and makes them the center of attention and concern. *Kofferay dibbi* is really a kind of sanctification ritual, not unlike the preliminary ceremonies of many Christian weddings, and altogether it is a happy occasion, marked by singing and dancing at the respective houses, in company with most of the guests who will attend the coming wedding. Since it is also the last night the boy and girl will spend as part of the largely unmarried set that is paying them court, *kofferay dibbi* has some of the bittersweet nostalgia of a graduation, a leaving behind of the familiar for a new status, as yet unexperienced.

Culminating the long days of parties, wedding announcements, and arrangements is the *bale dibi* (or actual wedding). All neighboring villagers and members of *nogs* within traveling distance assemble for the ceremony, which begins after the prayers at sundown and continues often through most of the night. The marriage contract (*ᶜaqd*) is written and signed (*katib el-kitab*) before the local *maᶜzoun*, a government-appointed, but locally selected village official. The *maᶜzoun* also asks for the consent of the bride and of the groom and officially registers the union.

Then comes the bestowal of gifts, which, in Nubia, is of special importance. At this time the boy receives shares in land, water wheels, date palms, cows, and even houses, as well as smaller gifts (*karray*). Gifts are given not only among the groom's new peers, the married men, but also by the older men, so the exchange relationship is established across generational lines. The sum of inherited shares and gift exchanges will determine whether the groom can support his new household *nog* in Nubia or must go to the city to supplement his income.

For this ceremony, the groom sits in a circle of men, and a man with a book sits next to him to register the gifts. First the gifts of family heads are offered, the act marking the young man as now able to reciprocate in this adult activity and tying him ceremoniously to a pattern of reciprocal exchanges from which he may never be free as long as he remains part of the community. After the gifts of neighbors and less closely related members of the *nogs* are recorded, the father of the groom will stand up and ceremoniously declare what he is bestowing on his son. "I give my son my share in the Fagirob *eskalay*," he may say. This will have been a matter of previous discussion, for often the father of the bride is then prepared to say, "And I give my daughter my share in the same *eskalay*." Following this exchange, the bride's brother may return a small share in the same *eskalay* that he received when getting married. A maternal uncle may say, "I give my sister's son a quarter of such and such cow." Even a house no longer in use may be given a groom, though this is less usual. Hopefully, the new couple will receive enough to begin life as a *nog*. More importantly, the groom is henceforth a man. Even if his father continues to enjoy authority over his son, the new groom, say the Nubians, "feels differently now about the land he tills; it is his own."

While the men are offering their *karray* outside, the women gather in the house for a similar ceremony. The shares in water wheels, land, cows, and houses are echoed in the jewelry now bestowed upon the bride by her mother and by others of her mother's generation who love her and are close to her. Ideally, most of the gold worn by a married woman should come to the bride from her groom, but the groom's mother, the bride's mother, and the bride's maternal aunts are expected to make generous contributions. No Nubian bride leaves this prenuptial party without enough personal adornment in gold and silver to signify that she has reached adulthood. Gold earrings, ankle bracelets, pendants, necklaces, and hair ornaments are presented; the pieces that the groom offers may be new, but the gifts of the bride's mother, mother-in-law, and aunts are often older pieces, the legacy that one generation of women passes on to the next, not as a blind inheritance but as a gift at the time of attaining adulthood. The jewelry is a gift given in such a way as to remain, like the communities' agrarian resources, active and in use, not put away and neglected because inherited by a woman who has left the community to live an Egyptian life in Cairo. The jewelry, which is the bride's personal property, may save the woman or her children from disaster in the extremities of financial hardship.

The bride also receives small gifts of money, food, and such household objects as woven colored plates as *karray* from her sisters, her brothers' wives, and her friends, as well as from her mother's friends and neighbors and from distant female relatives of both bride and groom. These *karray* serve to establish, for the bride, those ties of reciprocity by which she, too, will be bound as long as she lives in the community.

After the ceremony of the bestowal of wealth and *karray* the dancing and singing resumes, as in the following description of a Fedija wedding:

Boom! Boom! Boom!
    The drumbeats were louder, the stars winking, the lanterns flickering red in the sand, the brush fires lighted and held up in handfuls to tighten with heat the skin of the great drums. Every night since the cleaning of the grain and the signing of the marriage contract there had been dancing, but this, the wedding night, was the most important, the climax of the ceremony. Every able-bodied man in the village moved in the huge circle on the sand. They clapped for the measured line dance, a shuffle

[1] Elizabeth Warnock Fernea, *A view of the Nile*, p. 221.

back and forth, the circle of men weaving back and forth on the sand, singing as they moved.
    The women danced behind, in groups of four and five, in twos and threes, their hands locked together at their sides, red-and-gold-striped silk scarves tossed over their black veiled heads. So measured and controlled was their dance that the loose silk scarves never slipped, but only moved as they moved, to the drumbeat and the singing. Gold gleamed in the firelight, with the fine-boned brown faces, the white teeth, the white drums held high, boom, boom, boom above the white turbans, the white gullabiyas, the brilliant silk scarves floating. The people of the village were dancing, dancing on the sand.[1]

At some point later in the evening the groom leaves the guests and is danced to his bride, who, dressed in her marriage finery, waits in the *diwani*, or marriage room of her own home, which has been specially decorated for the occasion. Heading the festive procession (*seefa*) is the village chanter, or "forever" man, who, accompanied by drums, sings an ancient marriage song; between stanzas, the "forever" man will intersperse long lists of the bride's ancestors and the groom's ancestors and will recite couplets in praise of the families now being united.

At the bride's house, the procession disperses and the guests return to the dancing and singing. A few children may remain behind to peer through cracks in the roof and try to observe the contest of wills inside the *diwani*.

The groom, as in other parts of Egypt and most of the Middle East, is expected to keep giving his new bride small presents to persuade her to speak to him. When the bride speaks for the first time, the children leave and the couple may then proceed to consummate their union; occasionally a midwife's assistance is necessary, for the practice of female circumcision makes initial sexual experience very difficult. This particular custom seems inexplicably cruel in a society notable for its lack of cruelty. Yet it is practiced by women on their young daughters and they believe that it is necessary to the proper raising of a girl, helping her, the women say, to act with a degree of self-control that saves both her and the community from trouble. Small wonder, however, that the marriage night is a very tense period for many couples.

The belief that a bride should come to her husband untouched by other men is as strong in Nubia as in neighboring lands. Yet, if a Nubian bride is discovered not to be a virgin, no violence erupts as is sometimes the case in Arab communities; Nubian society takes care of the problem in other ways. Among Fedija Nubians, a girl who brings this social misfortune upon herself and her family must quickly be married by a paternal cousin, even if he is already married. The cousin must be someone who will care for the girl and will agree never to mention the reason for their marriage or taunt the girl with her past mistake. This is stated as ideal behavior; killing or mistreating the girl in any way is neither expected nor condoned.

A man is married in his bride's home and, throughout Nubia, spends some time there, depending on local custom; forty days is frequently reported as the average period. After the first seven days, when neither the bride nor the groom are supposed to leave the *diwani*, the groom may visit all his bride's neighbors briefly and take his ease in her community. During this time the wife theoretically learns how to serve her husband; she has long ago acquired the skills of cooking and housekeeping, but managing a husband is a new task, which, the Nubians say, must be learned individually, for it is different with each couple. The bride is better able to develop ability in this realm while she is in the accustomed familiarity of her own home; better, too, for her to become acquainted with her new husband in the security of her own territory, rather than in that of her mother-in-law. After this initial honeymoon period, the couple usually goes to the groom's father's house, sometimes to live there for months, sometimes for years, depending on a great many economic and social circumstances. Studies of current household composition show that most nuclear families have their own house, but some say this was less true in the past.

Shortly after returning to his home with his new bride, the young groom may have to go to Cairo or another distant city to earn his living and support his new family. Many Nubians divided their energies, spending some years as farmers and some years as urban employees, but opportunities to return to Nubia and earn a living in agriculture were few, particularly if a man lacked the means or desire to begin his married life in this way. Men who returned either brought an income with them from outside the community (savings, a pension) or were accepted as dependents in the home of a kinsman.

Marriage, then, economically, socially, and ceremonially, is the most momentous occasion in the life of a Nubian man or woman. Rich and elaborate in detail and execution, the ceremony involves the entire community and serves to focus and reemphasize the basic needs and values of the family and, ultimately, the community.

The practice of bestowing wealth on the groom at the time of marriage has social as well as economic significance and serves also as a tension-reducing aspect of Nubian culture. In many peasant communities, the father's stranglehold on land appears to be the cause of much hostility between generations; the sons are often deprived not only of a home of their own, but also of the means of subsistence until they are middle-aged. Even when the father dies, the eldest son usually inherits the greater portion, and the other sons are left with inadequate land; troubles between brothers over inheritance are commonplace. But in Nubia, the issue of the patrimony is settled at the outset of a man's adulthood; in a large family, one or two sons may be provided for, and the remaining sons know early that they will be obliged to leave and work in the cities. Thus, the bitterness is kept to a minimum. Some property retained by the father is, of course, inherited and subject to the equal division among heirs prescribed in Shari'a law. But this may involve no more than the family house, since the rest of the property has already been assigned to its next owner.

Only if a father feels doubtful about the seriousness of his son's marriage is he likely to avoid giving him much property. Such a public statement of doubt is itself unsettling to a marriage and may eventually be a self-fulfilling prophecy. Older men do keep a hand in their son's agricultural activities, but only, say the Nubians, through custom and with respect; the community considers shameful any failure by a father to bestow on a marrying son as much of a share in the family holdings as seems practical and possible at the time.

Flexibility, then, is inherent in the Nubian system of sharing the ownership of resources. Flexibility is also evident in the system of dividing the ownership of land between generations. A man, by giving land to his son or daughter, unites shares and creates a large enough holding to support or help support a new family group. Only by such rational manipulation of resources can control of the land be managed in order to assure continual use. By choosing young men with serious intent and apparent attachment to Nubian values and society, and by bestowing land upon them at the time of marriage, the society assures that the *eskalays* and the palm trees will not fall into disuse either through arguments about ownership or because too many heirs, with too small interests, are unwilling to cooperate in arranging for the land's management and utilization. No arbitrary rule of inheritance could guarantee this result as well.

The Nubian marriage illustrates still another dimension of social relations between members of the same community—the dyadic, reciprocal relationships established among men and women by the *karray*, or exchanges of gifts and material assistance. Through these dyadic exchanges among peers the resources of the community can be further employed to provide for the particular, often sudden crises in the lives of individual members. Through *karray*, the houses are replastered, the fields are harvested, and banquets are provided for large numbers of guests. This relationship is explicitly recognized and clearly stated; those who fail to assume their responsibility in such tasks are ostracized. Thus, while the individual is doing his duty toward someone to whom he is obligated or whom he wishes to obligate, the cumulative effect is of general

consequence, since this is the manner in which the community mobilizes its efforts to produce ceremonies and to complete difficult tasks that involve everyone.

The Nubians, in their very conscious willingness to accept the privileges and obligations of exchange relationships with many other people and for many purposes, are utilizing one of the most potent forces for social unity to which we have recourse. In many societies today, exchanges are no longer an effective force in neighborhood or community affairs, being sporadic and individual rather than organized and general. The Nubians have perhaps gone a step further in reciprocity and added a ceremonial component to such behavior.

"We are all attached to each other like the links of a chain," said one Nubian, "and at the moment when something must be accomplished, the links are pulled tightly together." The circles within which the links are pulled together may involve neighbors, members of the village, members of the household *nog*, the intermediate *nog*, or the largest *nog* of extended kinsmen. Friendship is the least formalized circle and may be the smallest. "If my neighbor comes without being asked when my roof must be replaced," says the Nubian, "that is how I know he is my friend." The largest circles of reciprocity are stated in the wedding ceremonialism when the *karrays* are carefully recorded in lists and in public announcement. But, small or large, formal or less formal, the fundamental principle of the circles of exchange relationships remains the same—one of compelling and total reciprocity.

6. The Kenuzi Saint Cult

The Kenuz of northern Nubia, who comprise nearly half of the total Egyptian Nubian population, have adapted their culture to conditions of extreme scarcity of village resources. At the same time they have preserved a form of social organization that no longer has the important economic functions that were presumably once a major raison d'être. Fortunately, the anthropologist Charles Callender lived in a Kenuzi Nubian district for nearly a year with a group of research assistants. Here I largely depend on information from his papers and those of his assistants.

Earlier, I mentioned that the social structure of the Kenuz differs from that of the Fedija. The Kenuz are organized in patrilineally determined tribes closely resembling those of the nomadic Arabs. While adherence to a genealogical model involving calculations of descent from a founding ancestor is of greater apparent concern to the Kenuz than to the Fedija, the differences between the two groups on this basis should not be overemphasized. "In theory, a Kenuzi tribe is a patrilineal lineage descended from a single ancestor. The tribe, or maximal lineage, is divided into major lineages descended from sons of the ancestor. A major lineage in turn reproduces the structure of the tribe itself through divi-

sions into minor lineages, which tend to develop minimal lineages." However, says Callender, "much of this structure is simply a convention."[1]

The proliferation of lineage segments is counterbalanced by the incorporation of individuals and even whole lineages into another lineage through intermarriages and common residence. Thus, like the Fedija *nog*, the Kenuzi *gabila*, or tribe, is composed of permeable units into which individuals, unrelated by common descent, can pass. Their descendants will eventually be accepted as blood kinsmen. Basically, the Kenuz differ from the Fedija in their greater preoccupation with the ideological aspects of patrilineal descent, rather than in the social reality of their kinship organization. The strength of a Kenuz's dedication to and involvement with this subtribe is not affected by the fact that the genealogy determining this membership is at least as much ideological as genetic. Unlike the Fedija, tribal leaders among the Kenuz are formally recognized at the various levels of tribal division, and disputes are formally adjudicated according to the tribal relationship between the individuals involved. This de-

[1] Charles Callender, "The Mehannab: A Kenuz tribe," in *Contemporary Egyptian Nubia*, ed. Robert A. Fernea, II, 186–187.

gree of formal segmentation is missing among the Fedija, and disputes are not so apt to divide the communities into opposing camps on the basis of lineage divisions.

The strength of the Kenuzi tribal organization is dramatically illustrated in the activities of the *moulid*, or saint cult, which is highly developed among the Kenuz but totally lacking among the Fedija Nubians. While serving religious and personal ends, such cults also help to articulate and symbolize the tribal organization and its component parts.

In the Kenuzi district of Dahmit approximately 150 shrines of various importance were located, among a resident population of less than fifteen hundred persons. Some of these shrines, physically no more than a pile of stones, were the object of attention by a family, a single woman, or sometimes even children, who would imitate their elders by acting out cult activities as a form of play. The most important involved the entire tribe, while the lesser cults were associated with minor lineages of much more limited membership. Dr. Callender offers the following description of the major saint cult associated with one entire Kenuzi tribe.

The Mehannab sheikhs are Hassan and Hussein, regarded as the tribe's ancestors even though descent is traced only to Hassan—an irregularity probably connected with the prevalence of twins as the objects of tribal cults in East Dahmit. Their shrine, a small two domed building, stands on the outskirts of Jama [a village], next to a dancing ground and adjoining the tribal graveyard. The association of cemetery and shrine, reinforcing the ancestral motive prominent in tribal cults, formerly characterized other tribal shrines in Dahmit and can be seen in the ruins of the old Jama flooded in 1933.

Some aspects of the cult of Hassan and Hussein continue throughout the year. Women vow gifts to to the sheikhs if their requests are fulfilled; grooms visit the shrine during the wedding procession, and visits are made by persons leaving for Egypt. This annual climax of the cult is the *mulid* [saint's day celebration] held on the 15th of the Islamic month of Shaaban. This celebration is financed and produced by the tribe. Rather complex in nature, it combines such essentially secular activities as dancing and a feast with a minimum of ritual centering on the replacement of the tomb covers, which are carried in procession to the Nile for washing, and then paraded through the Mehannab villages.

Women present gifts to the shrine in fulfillment of vows made during the previous year, or for the privilege of dancing [although dancing may also be in fulfillment of a vow]. This mulid is the major tribal undertaking. Its integrating functions are clear: this event involves all the Mehannab in Dahmit [about 250 persons] and many of the migrants, some of whom return for the occasion or send gifts for vows made in Cairo or Alexandria.[2]

As is the case with many of the saint shrines of Nubia, the actual bodies of Hassan and Hussein are not presumed to lie buried at their cult tomb; rather the shrine is only symbolic of the burial place, even in the case of the minority of holy men who are presumed to have died in Nubia. The rising waters of the Nile reservoirs covered most of the area where shrines had been built before this century. The shrines of the more important saints often consisted of a whitewashed room with a dome on top, all constructed of stone and mud brick. Inside might be found an empty coffin with incense pots and candles, a fragment of an old antiquity, or a few slabs of rock. But whether elaborate or simple, the shrine sites were established on the basis of an *ishara*, or sign, often in a dream, to a person resident in the village.[3] The *ishara* indicated that the *baraka*, or blessed virtue of the deceased saint, might be manifested as miracles if a cenotaph were to be constructed at some particular location. Such dreams sometimes encouraged adults to take seriously the play shrines constructed by their children, and similar dreams dictated where shrines should be rebuilt after flooding. In every instance, however, the shrines are apt to disappear and the cults abort them unless they become the object of special interest of a particular tribal lineage or sublineage. Thus, of the 150 shrines found in Dahmit, only 12 had staffs appointed to care for them and only 7 were the object of saint's day celebrations.

While any shrine could be the object of a private vow and therefore of personal significance, the celebration of a *moulid* was usually the special responsibility of a lineage. Members of the lineage would provide food, in fulfillment of vows made on condition that some special wish be granted. In addition,

[2] Ibid., p. 204.
[3] Nawal el Messiri Nadim has most interestingly described the origins of these shrines in her M.A. thesis for the American University in Cairo, "The sheikh cult in Dahmit."

money was collected to help buy animals for the feast; these were the contribution of the entire tribal group.

Each important shrine had a *nakib*, or custodian, whose function was to collect and distribute to the needy the food left at the shrine, to oversee the planning and execution of the *moulid*, and to tend to the maintenance of the shrine. Such a prestigious position was usually passed from father to son and often was filled by the sheikh of the particular lineage involved. His female counterpart, the *nakiba*, was, however, usually selected by the *nakib* from among the needy women of the community. For her work in cleaning the shrine, lighting the candles, and filling the water jars outside the door, the *nakiba* was rewarded less by honor and more by material assistance through access to the food left at the shrine throughout the year.

In the earlier days of Nubian migration, when men had more freedom to come and go, Nubian migrants would return in large numbers for the *moulids* of their tribes, in some cases bringing new tomb covers with them, perhaps in imitation of the official Egyptian pilgrimage to Mecca each year, which involved carrying a new cover for the *ka^cba* (the Sacred Black Stone of Mecca). *Moulids* were, then, occasions when the urban and village components of the tribe united in support of a common enterprise. Friendly competition existed between the major tribal groups to see which one could produce the best feast and attract the most visitors, for, while it was the duty of the Kenuzi tribesman to attend and support his own *moulid*, it was his privilege to attend, as a guest, those of the other Kenuzi tribes. By the same token, vows could be made at any shrine, regardless of tribal affiliation; indeed, some shrines were specialized in the kind of *baraka* they offered, as in the case of one that offered special protection against scorpions in an area where they were thought to be particularly numerous.

The degree to which the saints' shrines served as the focal point for the rituals of lineage is illustrated not only by the inclusive joint celebration of the annual *moulid*, but also by the number of more private acts associated with the shrine. In addition to vows, which could be made at the shrine at any time of need, a bride visited the shrine on the morning of her wedding, often leaving an offering; each wedding procession stopped at the shrine, to leave a gift for the *nakiba*, together with white flags dipped in henna, similar to the flags often placed over the lintel of the new bride's room. Pieces of such flags could later be used as charms, along with some dust from the shrine, by other mothers who were hoping for a marriage for their own daughters.

Just as a Fedija Nubian ceremoniously takes leave of each household in the village when he leaves for the city and greets each household when he returns, so do the Kenuz visit their shrine, say a sura from the Quran for their revered sheikh, and leave a small offering. This visit is considered necessary because the *baraka* of the saint is believed to protect those absent from the village and working in the cities far away.

The great annual *moulids*, however, those joyous celebrations that involved the larger community, were held only at those important shrines among the Kenuz that are symbolic of the burial place of a founding ancestor of the tribe or subtribe. Colorful processions from shore to shrine, offerings of food, prayers, dancing, singing, and feasting were all to honor the founding ancestor, to seek his blessing and protection. In this sense, the saint cults are also ancestor cults, both lending symbolic importance to the ideology of tribalism and reinforcing tribal unity through providing a focus for joint rituals. With such minor exceptions as burial grounds and tribal guesthouses, this is all the Kenuzi tribe or its divisions can share, since water wheels and palm trees have almost disappeared and most of the agricultural land was under water much of the year from the beginning of the Aswan dams in 1901. Callender reports that, of the Mehannab tribes, about 1,000 members lived in Alexandria, 350 in Cairo, perhaps 100 in Aswan, and a few were scattered elsewhere; only 226 Mehannab were resident in Nubia at the time of the study.[4] How appropriate, then, to have as a symbol of tribal unity and a focus of tribal activity a saint whose *baraka* is limited neither by time nor by space!

What of the conditions in the Kenuzi districts before the first dam began to flood the region? Callender emphasizes the importance of tribal ownership of property stressed in the reports of the old days by his informants. "Land and water rights in a *saqia* [water wheel] development, acquired by an

---

[4] Callender, "The Mehannab," p. 183.

The *moulid* was an occasion for prayers and for the ceremonial changing of the shrine cover.
Flags decorated the area from riverbank to shrine.

Mothers and daughters dressed in their best for the festivities of the *moulids*.

individual, eventually passed by inheritance to a lineage, whose rights were ultimately conceptualized as ownership by the tribe, even though most Mehannabs had no rights in the saqias."[5] One wonders whether such corporate ownership would not eventually have had effects on the tribal lineage system not unlike those described in the case of the Fedija *nogs*. Ownership passes to individuals and in passing, through the random accidents of birth and death and the more deliberate acts of marriage, moves across lineage lines, involving men in lineages other than their own as determined by patrilineal descent. Unless property rights were totally corporate, belonging to the lineage or the tribe with no inheritable rights of private ownership, it is difficult to see how those property rights could have continued to conform perfectly to the strict tribal constructs that now prevail among the Kenuz.

Tribal membership among the Kenuz was also used as the basis for the formation of urban clubs, which, as we shall see, were of great importance in helping the migrant Nubians adjust successfully to life in cities. As Callender notes,

> Labor migration among the Kenuz preceded the building of the first dam at Aswan, although its earlier extent is uncertain. It may be a very old practice. Possibly the tribal system, or some of its aspects, may represent a means of adjusting to unsettled conditions; and perhaps the Kenuz should be viewed as practicing a form of nomadism, represented today by labor migration and formerly by riverine trade through which small settlements were often established in other areas. But an important element of stability during at least the past two centuries has been the role of Dahmit and the other districts as the tribal center, which it has held in spite of increasing depopulation.[6]

When we ask why a greater emphasis on tribalism is found among the Kenuz than among the Fedija Nubians, why the saint cults are celebrated in Kenuzi Nubia and not in the Fedija area, we are confronted with a problem familiar to students of human societies. Is it because the Kenuz were tribally organized by an Arab tribe centuries ago? Is it because saint cults keep tribal divisions strong, replacing, in a sense, property rights that might have had contrary effects? Or did saint cults with elements of ancestor worship develop among the Kenuz because they already possessed a strong tribal ideology? Historically, tribal shrines were found throughout Arabia long before the advent of Islam and were one of the manifestations of polytheism that the Prophet Mohammed attacked and destroyed when uniting his pantribal followers under one God. Yet one must remember that such worship conformed well with the conditions of a nomadic life, providing foci of common activity and belief for an otherwise dispersed population.

We do not need to choose between history and economic conditions as *the* primary cause for the development of Kenuzi saint cults and tribal institutions. We may merely recognize that these social institutions have served the Kenuz well in their struggle to replace their village resources with urban incomes, while enjoying the relative security of remaining part of something greater and more enduring than either the individual or his immediate family.

[5] Ibid., p. 207. [6] Ibid., pp. 214–215.

7. Migration and the Urban Experience

The period from the end of Turkish rule until the construction of the first Aswan Dam constituted a brief golden age of Nubian culture. However, beginning at the turn of the century, Nubian lands were progressively flooded by the reservoir of the Aswan Dam, which had been heightened several times by the British and the Egyptians. The new-found security, which probably resulted in a growth of the Nubian population, was undermined by a decline in the resource base, and ever greater numbers of Nubian men were thus obliged to seek employment outside Nubia in the cities of Egypt and the Sudan during the first half of this century. This pattern of migration was not totally unprecedented, since ample evidence exists to show that Nubians had sought urban employment before the twentieth century. What is remarkable is the way in which the Nubians managed to adapt to the economic necessity of migration and divided communities and still maintain the fabric of their society.

The way in which the Nubians found a footing in Egyptian urban society and in effect saved their rural villages from starvation, the way they were able to maintain their homeland when it was no longer able to maintain them, is intimately related to the nature of nineteenth- and early twentieth-century Egypt, a society then in transition from slaveholding to free labor. Although the British formally outlawed the slave trade in Egypt in 1880, the manumission of slaves took many years, and, informally, the social status of slave did not disappear until well into the twentieth century, when the last of the legally freed slaves died as retainers in their ex-masters' households.

While slaves were used for agricultural labor at various times and places in Egyptian history, in general the Egyptian agrarian economy depended more on sharecropping than on slave labor, as contrasted to the American South. In Egypt slaves were more usually a feature of wealthy households, a mark of distinction between the rich and the poor, the aristocrat and the common man. Even today, a Nubian doorkeeper is a sign of prestige among well-to-do Egyptians, even if he is shared with a dozen other families in an expensive apartment house; this standard seems to have been established during the period of slavery.

Raised in Egyptian households, the Nubian boys captured in slave raids were lost to their own culture. While the memories of slave raids are kept alive among Nubians today through frightening stories told by grandfathers, no tales are recorded that describe the restoration of a slave to his own family. Villages with many black inhabitants supposedly are found on the delta today, near Tanta, for example. Yet, little contact takes place between the contemporary Nubians and descendants of freed black slaves.

The first waves of migrants from Nubian villages, then, did not gain access to their initial posts as servants through the influence of slave ancestors. More likely, the middle- and upper-class Egyptian discovered that paying a black man, newly arrived in Cairo, a small sum to stand before one's door or to run errands was an attractive and logical substitute for the owning of slaves, which became legally difficult and hence far more costly toward the end of the nineteenth century.

This was a period of prosperity in Egypt. The price of Egyptian cotton on the world market increased greatly during the American Civil War, and at about the same time the tourist trade emerged as a source of income for the country. Upper-class Europeans discovered in Egypt not only a promising area for economic exploitation, but also a warm winter spa filled with entrancing antiquities. With the aid of foreign investment and guidance, luxurious hotels and restaurants were constructed to encourage and accommodate this new source of wealth. Egypt suddenly became a favorite stop on the world tours of the fashionable and wealthy.

Upon this scene appeared the first Nubian migrants. Like the blacks in America, Nubians were associated with slavery and servitude in the public mind and were considered particularly suitable for this work. Without special training, with often only fragmentary knowledge of Arabic, they still found ready employment as servants in the strata of Egyptian society enjoying new prosperity. The Nubians provided the trappings of the old aristocratic, slave-owning wealth, but did so as free men who could leave their jobs at will to pay visits to their native villages. Tall, handsome, proud, and dignified, they had not experienced the humiliations of slavery and were hired not only by private families, but also by the new foreign hotel keepers, who provided long gold-braided robes, tarbushes, and snowy turbans for the Nubians in order to appeal to the Arabian Nights fantasies of the tourists and colonialists who thronged to Egypt at this time.

While seeing the Nubians as servants appealed to existing prejudices in Egyptian society, and while the Nubians' imperfect knowledge of Arabic encouraged attitudes of superiority on the part of Egyptians, the fact that the Nubians were Muslim automatically gave them a legal status in the society that could not be denied. The Nubians took care to emphasize the common denominator of faith by observing Islamic religious practices and by taking an interest in religious matters. At the same time, the Egyptian prejudice toward the *barabara*, as they called the Nubians, encouraged the Nubians to work and live together, avoiding all but the necessary social contacts with most Egyptians. As soon as a Nubian found a position he took care to try and fill the other jobs around him with men from his own community, and, if he left for Nubia, he replaced himself with another Nubian.

The jobs themselves, of doorman or house servants, required little formal skill and could be taken and abandoned with ease. The role of doorman in particular suited the Nubian temperament, for a doorman is frequently a neutral figure on the Egyptian scene and is often called upon to arbitrate quarrels between the other servants in a house or between lesser employees in a hotel. A good doorman comes to occupy a pivotal position in the affairs of a house, an apartment building, or a hotel, even today, after a century of change in Egypt, and the householder or building manager, who is himself frequently absent, counts upon the general knowledge that the Nubian doorman has acquired to help him keep the establishment successful and at peace. The role of doorman was also an excellent way of infiltrating Nubians into other jobs within the household, and the doorman often was instrumental in helping his fellow Nubians gain positions as waiters or cooks or drivers.

Nubians use the term "adventurer" to describe their great-great-grandfathers who first went to the cities of Egypt to look for work. Going to the city was, and remains, a great adventure for the village boy, just as for any country folk. The city is a risky place where one may experience great success or crushing failure, where temptations are plentiful and rewards often ephemeral. A young man's relatives in the village always had ambivalent attitudes toward the adventure, for, although the work provided much-needed income, it also offered an opportunity for the young man to meet and marry an

Egyptian woman and perhaps disappear forever from the Nubian scene. (In Egypt any prejudice against the Nubian black is largely impersonal in character and quickly becomes irrelevant as soon as one becomes directly acquainted with a particular Nubian; the virtue of a steady job has made many Nubians most acceptable husbands for Egyptian women.)

Linguistic, racial, and cultural differences between Nubians and city Egyptians should not be unduly stressed, however, in explaining the Nubian group cohesion in urban centers; in many ways the Nubians were doing no more than other ethnic and kin groups in the same setting. At all levels of Middle Eastern society, even today, the extended family is expected to help in locating work, and the monopolization of particular jobs by certain religious or ethnic groups is a well-known historical phenomenon.

In establishing themselves in the cities of Egypt in the twentieth century, the Nubians were doubly fortunate. Not only were they replacing in part a labor force, slaves, that had suddenly disappeared, but they also were entering the urban scene just when the economy was expanding to create ever-higher levels of demand for workers in the service occupations. Thus, the Nubians did not have to compete for traditional occupations already preempted by other groups, and they constituted one of the few lower-income groups that directly benefited from the new tourist trade and from the expenditures of the new foreign population and the growing Egyptian upper middle class. The Nubians' success in establishing themselves as part of the urban labor force, then, would not be so remarkable except for two factors: the degree to which the majority of Nubians remained associated with their ancestral villages over several generations, and the rapid upwardly mobile movement of their position in the urban employment scene.

The change that has occurred in the Nubians' position in the urban labor market in Egypt is a phenomenon that cannot be easily considered as common to all groups in an expanding economy. Egyptians and resident foreigners still generally believe that Nubians work almost exclusively in the service sector of the economy. Indeed, the great majority of Nubians do, but the last two decades have changed the pattern significantly.

In 1962 a survey was made of approximately 1,000 migrant Nubians who were identified and located on the basis of a survey of households conducted in Nubia itself.[1] The selection was carefully made in order to ensure a representative sample of the estimated 100,000 Nubians who reside outside their ancestral villages. The survey revealed, among other things, that the Nubian employment profile, when compared with the total distribution of all Egyptians in various job categories, was almost identical with that of the population at large. In other words, for the size of their population, the Nubians are represented equally with Egyptians in the professions, in managerial positions, and as white-collar workers. When one considers that the Nubians entered the Egyptian urban economy in force only slightly more than fifty years ago, and that at the time they were illiterate, did not speak Arabic, and had low ascribed social status outside their own lands—their achievements deserve and require some further examination.

The reasons for this rapid upward mobility lie partly in the conditions of Egyptian urban life, as the Nubians experienced them, and partly in the fact of being Nubian. Certainly, the association with foreigners was one such condition. Many older Nubians state a preference for employment in foreign homes or establishments. This action may be partly attributed to a Nubian sensitivity about the Egyptians' attitudes toward him, but it is also true that foreigners, with egalitarian ideas and bad consciences following the end of slavery, may have treated Nubians with greater respect and relied on them more than the ordinary Egyptian employer would have done. In any household or business enterprise in a foreign land, the local employee is far more than simply a man doing a job; he is also a channel of communication between the foreigner and the local environment. The local employee must cope with much that his employer only half understands and must explain why some actions are appropriate and others are not. Enterprising Nubians, who quickly learned at least the rudiments of the foreign employer's language, were local citizens

[1] The survey was conducted by Dr. Peter Geiser, and his bibliography should be consulted for more detailed analyses of the subject ("Some impressions concerning the nature and extent of stabilization and urbanization in Nubia society," in *Contemporary Egyptian Nubia*, ed. Robert A. Fernea, I, 143–169).

who were able to guide the foreigner through the often bewildering labyrinth of daily affairs, whether it involved food supplies, government regulations, or street demonstrations.

In return, the foreigner paid his Nubian servant higher wages and, prompted by a variety of motives, sometimes helped the man to bring his family to Cairo and to place his sons in school. At the turn of the century the number of foreign schools was increasing in Egypt, schools that often accepted a few tuition-free students, especially if the student's father worked for a foreigner known to the school. Servants' quarters were sometimes large enough to house employees' families, and so Nubians were able to find a place in the city for their children at less expense than that of other rural migrants in similar positions.

Thus, the symbiosis between the Nubian and the foreigner in private homes and public establishments, though by no means the exclusive involvement of the city Nubians, was of considerable reciprocal advantage. Aside from the economic benefits, the fact that the Nubian, like the foreigner, was also considered something of an outsider may have contributed an element of sympathy and understanding to the employer-employee relationship. In strictly economic terms the Nubian was simply a salaried employee, but in a broader context the job was more all-encompassing, even if the foreigner was not always aware of this. The act of cooking and serving food to guests in Nubia, as throughout the Middle East, is an honorable one and brings credit upon the host. For a Nubian to be partly responsible for the well-being of guests, whether in a home or a hotel, was in accordance with his traditional values. The fact that Nubian men undertook kitchen tasks, which in their own homes would have been performed by women, did not upset the Nubian male as`it might an American, for instance; whatever doubts the Nubians have about their masculinity, they are not manifested in this way!

Furthermore, the foreigners' own values did not fail to make some impact on Nubian culture through several generations of relationship. The character of a good man, as defined by a Nubian, is not unlike a description of a proper nineteenth-century Puritan English gentleman. Honesty is very highly prized and frequently mentioned, as is the associated virtue of dependability. It would be ab-

surd to associate these virtues only with Nubians, as a category apart from other Middle Easterners, or to suggest that the qualities developed only through contact with foreigners. However, I cannot refrain from emphasizing that these virtues are *discussed* more by Nubians than by any other group of people I have met anywhere, not only in the Middle East.

By working in hotels and night clubs and in the homes of wealthy foreigners and Egyptians, the Nubians had an opportunity to observe life styles largely unfamiliar to other Egyptians of low social status. The Nubian sons who played with the children of their father's employer, may have aspired to identify themselves in the future with the employer's social group, an aspiration the Nubian fathers were quite ready to encourage. For, although working as a servant is no disgrace in the Middle East, white-collar jobs are more prestigious among Nubians as among other Egyptians, and one seldom encounters the attitude that what was good enough for a father is good enough for his son.

Why, then, under circumstances of increasing social mobility, did Nubians continue to be interested in village affairs? The old ties were there, but they might not have sufficed if new institutions had not been created to reinforce the links between migrants and their home villages. The Nubian *gamaʿiyya* society, or social club, was the urban institution that, more than any other, played a key role in the Nubians' struggle for a place in the city and in their upward mobility in the labor market. It was the *gamaʿiyya* that helped the migrants cope with the new problems of city life and assisted them in the task of maintaining close contact with their rural communities.

At one time or another between the end of the Second World War and the 1963 resettlement, more than forty *gamaʿiyyas* were active in Cairo, Alexandria, and Aswan. The successes of the *gamaʿiyyas* as well as their problems are reflected in a general history of the Cairo Fedija clubs from Tushka district, which has been reconstructed through personal accounts from many Nubians and especially from Hamza El Din, a celebrated Nubian musician and composer now teaching and recording in the United States.

Clubs like the *gamaʿiyyas* are at least as old as the mid-nineteenth century when guild lists from the time of Mohammad Ali record the existence of

Kenuzi Nubian associations among dock workers at Egyptian ports. Apparently, the Kenuz, armed with their experience at the port of Aswan near the First Cataract, made their way to other Egyptian cities well ahead of the more isolated Fedija peoples. When Hamza's grandfather, with other men from Tushka, migrated to Cairo in the early 1920's, they came by donkey and sailboat, attracted by the high wages and labor demand of the city, for no steamboats connected the Sudan and Egypt, or the villages between.

The *gama°iyyas* grew out of the migrant adventurers' desperate need for a meeting place where they could sit together and speak, in their own language, about their own affairs. Working as servants in European quarters of the city, which lacked suitable coffeehouses, the early migrants had to count on meeting their fellow Nubians in coffee shops near Abdine and other market centers of the city, between daily errands. The first formally organized Fedija clubs began in the twenties. Several men from the same largest *nog*, or maximum group of kinsmen with the same family name, each contributed a few piasters a month toward the rental of a room where all could meet. Similar arrangements persisted for several years, but eventually the basis for Fedija clubs shifted from *nog* to district of origin —the *nahia*, or collection of villages strung together along the narrow stretches of fertile Nile shore. Tribal membership, however, has remained the basis of Kenuzi urban clubs, yet another example of the greater strength of formal kinship as a basis for association among this tribally organized people.

During the twenties and thirties, older members of the Fedija migrant community were beginning to die in the city, and a common burial ground was needed. The men were also concerned at the time with the manner in which Nubian women traveled all over the city to pay traditional condolence calls on the occasion of a death. As we have seen, condolence calls at the mourning ceremonies are a strict obligation in Nubian society on the part of relatives, neighbors, and friends, and the Nubian migrant women took care to observe the custom, although the distances between houses were often greater than in Nubia and the territory through which they passed was not exclusively Nubian.

The men did not like the women traveling freely throughout the strange city, and they tried to stop the practice. The women refused, pointing out that Nubian women, just like Nubian men, needed the opportunity to console each other at the time of death, that they, too, had feelings and emotions, and that, if they were not permitted to visit each other's houses on these sorrowful occasions, they would each contribute money and rent a room for a woman's club! Such an ultimatum on the part of the womenfolk helped the men's clubs make their decision to buy the burial grounds, in the hope that this would be a common meeting place for both women and men. Many clubs purchased plots, which was a source of great relief to the resident city community, for Nubians attach much importance to the graves of their ancestors and regularly place offerings of water at the gravesides on religious holidays.

The clubs were also centers of communication and education. Lessons learned by the grandfathers during their first days in the city were passed on to sons and grandsons. Recipes were exchanged. Kin were recruited to provide extra service for important parties where Nubians were employed. Job openings were reported, and replacements were found from the same *nog* or village, for often news traveled by word of mouth from the villages to the city; the club was a convenient central headquarters at which the newcomers and the older residents could meet.

Teachers were hired in the 1930's and early forties to tutor the Nubian men and their young sons. To the Nubian adult of that period, education meant arithmetic, since the majority of men were faced with doing regular accounts as part of their jobs in private houses or in hotels. However, the sons enrolled in Cairo schools were also at a great disadvantage because of their comparative ignorance of Arabic. Thus, the reading and writing of Arabic was added to arithmetic, and these sessions became, in effect, adult literacy classes as the fathers listened to and participated in their sons' lessons.

"While we were servants at our work," said Hamza, "everyone wanted to be master in the club," and this led to difficulties, since "everyone talked and nobody listened." Sometimes a decision was reached only when, after hours of discussion and argument, the men departed, saying, "It's up to the rest of you." Eventually only the club president would be left and he would do as he thought best.

Despite the arguing and indecisiveness, the clubs in the forties were well enough organized to start food cooperatives, through which shipments of sugar, tea, and kerosene were sent to a number of their home communities. The mechanism of the cooperatives was later used to send government-subsidized rations of similar staples, including American surplus wheat, to the villages. Financial support for the cooperative was raised by selling shares to club members, and profits were divided and distributed annually in proportion to the size of the individual investment. The cooperative also provided a livelihood for a few adult men who preferred to live in Nubia but liked to visit Cairo occasionally for annual business meetings.

In the forties, the clubs built village elementary schools, which the Egyptian government then pledged to maintain and to supply with teachers. The schools were constructed with money sent from the cities and labor provided by men living in the villages. Many men had cash at the time, from compensation for land flooded by raisings of the Aswan dam. Wages were also good, particularly after the Second World War, when the British occupation of Cairo encouraged the opening of a number of new night clubs and restaurants. Here Nubians found employment as waiters, cooks, and, in some cases, managers.

During this period of prosperity, a growing tension between older and younger generations created some problems in the clubs. Many of the young men moved their social life to nearby coffee shops where they could drink tea and play backgammon without worrying about showing continual respect for their elders. In some cases, the loss of young members resulted in partial closing of the clubs. In other instances, compromises were reached whereby the youth were permitted to set up Ping-Pong tables, play backgammon, and enjoy themselves in the early evening, provided they replaced the furniture so the older men could relax more formally later on.

An interest in group sports among the young men also added new life to the clubs for a time. The younger men formed soccer teams to play matches in vacant lots and in city parks; they sold tickets to the matches to their adult relatives, who in turn became interested in the games. The younger and older generations pooled the ticket money to renovate the clubs and buy more recreational equipment.

But another, more serious development threatened the unity of the Nubian migrant communities in the forties and the fifties, when the third generation of Nubians was seeking employment in the city. By this time many Nubian men had profited from their father's ambitions for their education and had moved into white-collar jobs, the teaching and clerking positions to which their secondary education entitled them. A few with some years of college had achieved even higher job status. The new semiprofessional group of achievers was losing interest in the clubs, and this was a source of worry not only to the older men, but also for some of the youngest members. Why were the few educated men deserting the Nubian organizations?

Some members of the third generation, deeply concerned about a possible loss of Nubian culture and cohesion, formed groups to rejuvenate the arts of the Nubian past. A few talented young men, stimulated by Cairo city life but still feeling rooted in Nubian society, met in their spare time to paint, write poetry, and compose and play music. In this way, they hoped eventually to attract the interest and attention of the educated Nubians. They offered their services at weddings and began playing and singing in the evenings at the Nubian clubs. The Abu Simbel club was the first *gamaʿiyya* to welcome the young Nubian artist-performers, reports Hamza El Din, a member of the original group. (The people of Abu Simbel, he says, have a reputation for being artistic and interested in art, just as the people of Ballana are noted for their hard work.)

"But we never performed at the clubs of our own *nogs*," reports Hamza. "Such behavior would have shamed and humiliated our elders. And of course we could never perform in our own villages."

Yet, when they visited their own villages, the young men did perform, informally, for their mothers and sisters, who were pleased and excited to have their Arabic-speaking city-dwelling offspring come home to sing the old half-remembered Nubian songs of their childhood. The women prayed for the young men and encouraged their efforts in many small practical ways. Gradually, the music of tradition and nostalgia, sung with enthusiasm by a new generation, helped to reestablish the sense of pride in and the consciousness of being Nubian. Partly as a result, two new *gamaᶜiyyas* were formed, uniting all the Kenuz and Fedija in one large assembly; the youth were particularly enthusiastic about this development, which did not replace but merely supplemented the smaller district clubs and served to draw together the men from the two largest regions of Nubia.

Clearly, the institution of the Nubian clubs served important but different purposes for each generation of migrant workers. The first clubs offered a meeting place for lonely, often confused men dealing with the problems of a large, sophisticated city. Unity brought other benefits: the burial plots, the cooperatives, the schools for the villages that aided the new generation. The third generation, of which Hamza was a member, found the association of the clubs a basis for the development of talents that would have remained largely dormant in the villages. The arts have little place in Nubian society, except where they have a traditional purpose— decorating the houses, for example, or providing singing and dancing at weddings or *moulids*. Performing before one's elders in the villages would have been considered disrespectful except on such traditional occasions as weddings. Otherwise, playing instruments and singing was strictly a peer-group activity. But the young artists in the cities found men from other communities who were eager to convert the entertainment regularly enjoyed on Nubian ceremonial occasions to that of a regular pleasure, occupying and enriching one's leisure time. Interested in Nubia, but anxious also to demonstrate their new talents and sophistication, these young men found the performing of traditional Nubian music and the recitation of poetry an acceptable basis upon which they could find common ground with their more conservative, older, or better educated kinsmen.

The artistic and social revival in the Nubian clubs of the fifties and early sixties helped unite the migrants and enabled them more easily to face the crises of resettlement. Although the Nubians never became an effective political pressure group, individual clubs submitted many petitions to the various government ministries responsible for resettle-

ment and tried to gain public support for their cause in the press and among the influential artists on the radio and television stations. In return, the ministries used the clubs as a means of communicating with Nubians in Cairo. Perhaps any group of people threatened with loss of land and property becomes politically active, but the Nubians had an organized base from which they could maintain the essential ties between country and city while the society was in the process of traumatic change.

Just before the actual resettlement began in 1963, much traveling took place between village and city, and many adjustments of residence and shares were effected to ensure proper recording of property rights so that adequate compensation would be made by the government to each family and each *nog*. The unique share system of Nubia was not easily transferrable to the government information forms, and the interwoven patterns of interests in *eskalays*, cows, and date palms had to be carefully disentangled and converted into statements of private ownership and specific property, statements that tallied with those of one's neighbors and kinsmen. This process alone was the source of great anxiety, and the fact that the communities survived, without violence, such a potential source of conflict is a further example of the effectiveness of the Nubian polity.

Finally, the young group of performing artists served to unite the Nubian communities in still another way, by presenting benefit concerts. All proceeds from the sale of tickets to these several performances given in Cairo in 1962 and 1963 were donated to a resettlement fund—to aid the old, the sick, the disadvantaged in faraway Nubia as they prepared to move. The young artists' reputation and their appearances in one of Cairo's newest and most attractive theaters attracted not only crowds of Nubians, but also many interested Egyptians and foreigners, which helped draw public attention to the plight of the dislocated peoples and thus aided them in their appeals to government officials.

Nubian migration, as we have described it, emerges as a different phenomenon from much labor migration elsewhere in the world. Instead of separating the Nubian from his society, migration reinforced his ties to his culture. This was partly because migration among the Nubians was frequently a community rather than an individual decision. Men were destined to go to the city, on the basis of whether or not they received enough property to survive as agriculturalists in the home community. The duration of the migratory period varied also; a man might go for a few years before marriage and return to marry, sometimes even settling in the village at that time. He might remain in the city, if his land was insufficient, returning only on holiday every few years. He might eventually retire in Nubia, with a government pension for support, for example.

So long as the pattern remained one in which men left wives and children in the villages, their ties with the community stayed comparatively firm, reinforced by the clubs in the cities. In recent years increasingly large numbers of Nubian women have moved to Cairo or Alexandria or Aswan to live with their husbands, a fact that indicates a greater investment in life in the city than in the past. However, at the same time, the land in Nubia remained in use and the villages were occupied in almost exactly the same proportion of people to arable land as before the larger-scale migrations. All the women and children and older men left behind in the villages, unless they were too old or ill, contributed something to their own support. The movement of Nubian women to the cities was due in part to the fact that for many nothing was left to occupy them in their native villages.

Even for Nubians who had established household *nogs* in the cities, Nubia still remained for many a place of refuge where one went to recover from an illness or an occupational setback, a place where one hoped to retire one day. The "blessed country" remained a place of security and peace—in short, it was home, in the way that many Nubians feel Egypt can never be. Cairo, said the women, had its advantages, particularly if one needed medical care, but basically it was costly, dirty, and full of thieves. With very few exceptions, the women tried to return to Nubia when they were pregnant, "so the child can be born at home." With good Nubian air and family to help, the baby was bound to have a better chance of survival!

If the direction of change before resettlement had involved more and more migrations to the cities by Nubian women, the ability of Nubian culture to maintain itself in more-or-less traditional patterns

surely would have gradually diminished. At the time of resettlement, most Nubian women in the city were still uneducated and many did not know Arabic; thus, still speaking the mother tongue, they passed on to their children the traditions and values of the native communities in the language that best expressed them. Whether the village culture would have remained intact as the majority of Nubian women became partially assimilated into Egyptian urban society is questionable; at the time of resettlement this process was definitely underway.

During their time in the city, as we have noted, the Nubians were expected to return to the villages for feasts, such as the *moulids* in the Kenuzi region, or the weddings after the date harvest in the Fedija area; this returning became less possible in recent years, as Nubians became more formally committed to "better" jobs that required their presence for a set number of hours per day, a set number of days per year.

Such was the price Nubians were paying for their success in Cairo, and, had they not been obliged to pay it, the economic condition of their families and homeland would have suffered and their condition now would be far more difficult. As it is, many have jobs with great security and sufficient salaries to have been of key importance to the survival of many Nubian families during the difficult years of adjustment in Kom Ombo just after resettlement. Their history in the cities of Egypt is, then, no less remarkable than their culture in its traditional setting, and their record of urban adjustment compares favorably with that of European immigrants in the United States—though we customarily think of our history as somewhat unique in this respect.

The Nubian experience also demonstrates the narrowness of our belief that rapid change and adaptability is the special province of technological societies. The migrant worker changes his way of life because he is forced to by circumstance; he forgets his traditional culture because it is not applicable in the new community. This was simply not true of the Nubian, who took from the new situation only what he needed and wanted, and rejected the remaining elements in favor of his own values.

The experience did not traumatize but rather seems to have strengthened the Nubians as a group. In the words of the old proverb, "The fire that melts the butter makes the iron hard."

The existing structure of Nubian village communities provided the basis upon which men could organize in the city to cope with new sets of problems, for no social agency existed to take the place of this network of mutual aid. But it is more difficult to account so simply for the intelligence and openness that made the Nubian migrants quick to see and to take advantage of opportunities for bettering their condition, to learn foreign languages—along with foreign cooking and foreign customs—and, finally, to see many of their sons settled as doctors or bureaucrats in Cairo. From the cities and from their contact with foreigners they brought back to Nubia modified tastes in food, ideas for decorating and improving the construction of their houses, radios, and household items of metal and plastic. But, perhaps, because they also saw how little relation exists between contentment and material riches, they did not lose their people-centeredness, their belief that one of the best things in life is conversation and tea with one's friends or close relatives in comfortable, secure surroundings. For this, they have never found a place better than Nubia.

8. The Future

Today the Nubian homeland lies under the waters of Lake Nasser, the shores of which are inhospitable. If the Egyptian government had not undertaken a massive and costly effort to resettle the villagers together and provide them with land to cultivate near the town of Kom Ombo, the more than fifty thousand residents of Nubia would now be dispersed throughout Egypt, in the process of being transformed into an urban minority. For, without fragments of their society still living in villages, still observing traditional patterns of life, it is doubtful they would have survived long as a socially and culturally distinctive part of the urban scene. The villages kept the Nubian language alive, socialized the young children before they went to Cairo, and provided an environment that was a fundamental part of the children's cultural development. Villages remained the dependable check on the process of assimilation, the counterbalance to cities.

The survival of Nubian culture, then, would seem to depend on whether the villages of New Nubia will be able to provide the social functions of Old Nubia. In the new setting a great many circumstances of traditional village life have totally changed. The resettlement area is several miles from the Nile, so the river traffic of the feluccas is irrelevant and the river rituals can no longer be practiced. The isolation of the old communities is gone, for New Nubia is only a few minutes by bus from the towns of Kom Ombo and Aswan, situated on a broad treeless plain that lies in a region of Upper Egypt well suited to the growing of sugar cane. Rather than growing traditional millet and other grains, the Nubians are expected to cultivate sugar cane as their principal cash crop, with the help of canal irrigation and artificial fertilizers. *Eskalays* and cows have no place here. Although palm trees have been planted in Kom Ombo, many years must elapse before their fruit can provide that traditional source of wealth. Thus, several essential elements of both the economic and the ceremonial life of the Nubians are gone.

Of even greater significance is the increased contact between Nubian villagers and Egyptian administrators and institutions. Medical clinics, agricultural extension offices, and a variety of other facilities are a part of the every-day scene. All levels of schooling are available, and most Nubian children will be studying and speaking Arabic from the age of five or six. These factors, combined with the relative ease with which trips can be made to nearby towns, will eventually weaken the use of the Nubian language. Women, who had scarcely any need for Arabic in Nubia, will find themselves at a much greater disadvantage in this new setting. Within two or three generations, it is probable that only the eldest persons in New Nubia will be able to converse in the language of their forefathers.

On the other hand, as the quality of the new land improves, the villages of New Nubia will be far more viable economically than those of Old Nubia, and the pressure for men to migrate to the cities for work will be considerably reduced. According to the terms by which the Nubians were granted land, the beneficiaries are required to live in and cultivate the area themselves. In Old Nubia, pump irrigation projects opened in the 1940's to replace some of the land flooded by the first Aswan Dam, and the men were expected to stay and cultivate the land at that time. But many owners continued working in the cities under sharecropping arrangements whereby resident Nubians, together with a number of hired men from Upper Egypt, undertook the actual farming. This solution is technically illegal now, though reportedly a significant number of neighboring Egyptians are becoming involved in the cultivation of the new lands. More men are still actually present in Kom Ombo than in Old Nubia, and presumably the sex ratios will remain more balanced than in the past.

Perhaps the most positive factor for the future of a distinctive Nubian culture lies in the new range of interaction now possible among rural Nubians. A population once scattered in isolated settlements over two hundred miles along the banks of the Nile today lives in a tenth of that space. Families once separated for years are together again. Relatives who could only with great difficulty visit each other in different villages on special occasions may now do so by walking down the street. The young people, who previously looked forward to a large group of peers only upon moving to Cairo, have found many friends their own age in their own village settlements. In fact, one of the first problems that faced the Nubians after resettlement was that the attendance at ceremonial occasions, such as weddings, deaths, and *moulids* (which were quickly resumed in this new setting), attracted so many people that the food prepared for the feasts was totally inadequate! The ease of communication has had an almost intoxicating effect on younger people, help-

ing to counteract, to some degree, the traumatic shock of resettlement, which, of course, particularly affected the older Nubians.

In the twenties and thirties the growth of the migrant population in Cairo led to formation of the *gamaʿiyya* clubs, where opportunities arose for the development of artistic and other skills that would not have been possible in the old villages. Perhaps the new villages may experience a similar renaissance. We must remember that the sense of being "Nubian," rather than just a member of a particular tribe or village, has come only recently to this people. Recognition of the Nubians as a group with special rights and interests is also new on the national scene. Already, the Nubians have become aware of the advantage to be gained in remaining together rather than making their way individually. Within a few months of their resettlement, for example, they were able to dominate local elections for the National Assembly and to send Nubian delegates to Cairo.

The aesthetic qualities of Old Nubia—the view of the river, the village situation between mountains and water, surrounded by high green palm groves— were impressive to the outsider and were also much appreciated by the Nubians. But aesthetics are not necessarily the basis of a society. The isolation of the villages carried with the privacy a lack of many of the advantages urban Nubians came to appreciate, particularly medical care and education. Many young men (while seeking as many concessions as possible from the government at the time) regarded the resettlement as a positive step. In spite of all the initial difficulties, the Nubians did not feel altogether pessimistic about the new life they were to develop for themselves.

The Nubians are not, after all, to be compared with the American Indians, whose ways of life were so radically different from the Europeans who came to dominate their land that they were at an almost impossible disadvantage. The Nubians and the Egyptians are in many ways a single people, sharing the all-important fact of a common religious faith. Surely, as the years pass, the Nubian minority will come to share even more with the Egyptian majority. And, while we should be concerned for the future of this small minority, we should remember that in the mosaic of Middle Eastern life, many groups of people have retained their individuality and vitality for generations while living close to other groups distinct from themselves. I believe a Nubian society is likely to persist, for, until the still long distant day arrives when individual achievement and social mobility are the major factors in personal survival and success, bonds of kinship and group allegiance will remain relevant. Rather than indulge in romantic nostalgia for what is indisputably gone, we who care about the fate of this people must take pleasure in the fact that they are so well equipped by experience and circumstance to make the adjustments necessary for their survival. We can only hope that their attachment to what is culturally unique in their own heritage will find new expression among future generations of Nubian Egyptians.

NOTES ON NUBIAN ARCHITECTURE

by Horst Jaritz

Nubian architecture experienced a great renaissance in the first half of the twentieth century. The well-designed, spacious, and comfortable houses built of stone or mud, painted and decorated, with details executed in mud brick, excited the admiration of many Egyptian and foreign architects who traveled and worked in Nubia before the waters of Lake Nasser obliterated all traces of the villages.

The forms of Nubian architecture were a product of many factors. In examining the examples of house plans and photographs, we can see that the houses were designed with topography and climate as basic considerations, as well as the people's economic condition and social structure. In southern Nubia, home of the Fedija, enough land still remained in the twenties and thirties, when these houses were built, for people to cultivate and harvest dates as they had done in the past. On the higher banks above the river, the plateaus were still wide enough so that the Fedija could build and rebuild their houses, using older, inherited house plans, and the old east-west directional orientation, wherein the front of the house always faced the Nile. The area was still in reasonably good economic condition, and some masons, carpenters, and other house-building specialists still lived in the villages. All these factors help explain the greater size and generally better craftsmanship seen in the southern houses (A-type).

The northern, Kenuzi region was progressively flooded by the Nile after the building of the first Aswan dam. By the 1950's only a narrow, rocky strip between river and mountains remained of the originally much larger area of farmland and palm trees. The people were forced to move their houses back from the river several times, under rather difficult circumstances. The steep and rocky river banks prevented the people from rebuilding their houses on flat plateaus, with the old east-west orientation. The only possibility was to develop new plans and designs that would conform to the slopes of the banks, parallel to the river, that is, oriented north-south. A certain lack of unity in the plans and outer appearance of the northern (B-type) houses may be partly attributed to the difficult topographical situation. In addition, many of the northern artisans had been forced by circumstances to migrate to the cities for work, depriving the villages of certain kinds of skills and experiences.

Nubian houses, both northern (B-type) and southern (A-type), were designed carefully with the climate in mind. Winter months are quite cold with a steadily blowing north wind; hence, the living areas were placed to face south and west in order to receive as much sun as possible. On the other hand, because of the summer heat, which pours in from the south and west, the walls of the living areas were high, which created a shady patch close to the wall itself. For similar reasons, the loggias, or roofed open areas in the courtyard, were built on the south or east side of the courtyard and opened to the north and west in order to allow the best possible access to any breeze that came late in the evening. Arranged in this way, the loggias offered a more endurable living-and-sleeping area during the heat of the summers.

The climate was also responsible for the lack of windows in the family's private quarters. The highly placed narrow slits in the walls served to ventilate the rooms without exposing them to the cold winter winds. Another reason for the lack of windows was, of course, to keep the family out of the range of the neighbors, and especially the bad influences of the evil eye. Probably, there are also historic reasons for the lack of windows, since the desert tribes used to raid the settlements, robbing and attacking the villagers. This old threat may also be an explanation for the high walls of the compounds.

The importance of water to the Nubians cannot be exaggerated. In the southern houses, the *zirs*, or great clay water jars, were placed in the loggias, hung in wooden frames so the water might drip and cool in the shade; in northern Nubia, the frames were transformed into special small roofed "water huts," wherein the water jars were placed. The water huts opened either to the north, if they were attached to the courtyard's south wall, or to the north and south, to catch the passing wind, which helped to cool the water. The huts became a special architectural element in most northern (B-type) houses.

After the first dam was built, the supply of wood diminished along the northern Nile; this may account for the reintroduction of the mud-brick vaulted roof, which completely changed the architectural appearance of many northern villages. In the southern districts, however, where some agriculture was still possible, wood was still available for constructing flat roofs.

Mud also was in short supply in northern Nubia, as more and more of the previously fertile banks were covered; mud became so rare that it was carried up the rocky banks when the water level fell and was used as fertilizer on the stony ground, making small terraced gardens near the houses. Thus, field stone gradually replaced mud brick as the principal material for constructing walls. Nevertheless, small amounts of mud were still used for wall, window, and door decorations and for the construction of other complicated architectural detail work.

The Nubians' distinctive style of wall painting and executing mud relief has been described in detail in the literature. It should be pointed out, however, that in the south very little wall painting was employed to decorate the houses; mud-made relief work, simply, even austerely colored, was more common. That decoration and wall painting in particular were less important in the architecture of southern Nubia may be related to the fact that, in the south, nature still provided a colorful and beautiful background for life—in the palm groves, the orchards of mangoes and lemons, the flowering acacia trees, the green fields, and the golden sand. In the north, only rocks and sand were left, but, to replace the natural beauty, the arts of wall painting, house decoration, and colored mud relief suddenly flowered in the area. Motifs became considerably more varied and rich in detail, and the colorful houses stood on the dull and barren rocks almost as a challenge, as though the people responded to the hostile world of nature by creating another and more beautiful world of their own invention.

Types of Houses in Egyptian Nubia

Some idea of modern Nubian architecture can be gained from the plans and descriptions of thirteen houses surveyed in 1964–65 in Egyptian Nubia, even though the sample is geographically limited and includes only houses constructed during the last thirty years before the High Dam.

Undoubtedly, the layout of the rooms, the methods of construction, and some of the decoration may be traced to an older tradition. As, until the dam building began, conditions of life probably had not changed much for a very long time in this isolated part of the world, older ideas about architecture may not have been modified a great deal.

One of the most prominent forms found in the traditional architecture was the barrel-vaulted roof. Dating back to Pharaonic Egyptian times, when it had already been introduced into Nubia, we find such roofs in the funeral architecture during Meroitic and X-Group times. Later, barrel vaults spread over all of Christian Nubia and were used to roof both churches and houses.

After the Muslim invasion, barrel vaults seem to have disappeared from almost all parts of the country except the area from Daraw to Wadi el-Arab—north and south of the First Cataract, where the Kenuzi tribe had settled. However, in the years before the building of the Old Dam at Aswan (1902–1912), the vaulted roofs were not as common as one would suppose. At the moment when the rising water forced the population to leave their houses and to build new ones on higher levels, this type of construction suddenly reappeared. For, as wood for roofing became less available, builders had to rely on the old method of vaulting rooms with bricks made of sun-dried Nile mud. Help was drawn from Daraw, some twenty miles north of Aswan, where the roof type and the knowledge of its construction had survived. Specially prepared mud bricks measuring about 25 x 15 x 5 cm, with more straw than usual for lightness, and mud as the mortar, were the only building materials necessary.

The two side walls of a room were built to a height where they served as the vault's imposts; the one end wall rose to a height that usually was at least slightly greater than the arch's apex. When these three walls were completed, the masons started outlining, roughly, with mud, the vault's parabolic form against the end wall. They then began laying brick by brick against the supporting end wall until, after five or six courses, the inclined arch closed for the first time. Standing on a couple of planks across the side walls (which could be about nine feet apart), the masons continued the arching brick laying until the vault reached the front of the room, without the need of scaffolding, centering, or drawing. All the work was controlled by the eye and the experience of the individual mason.

Two main types of houses were common in Egyptian Nubia. One, the "cubiform mud-brick house with flat roof" and east-west orientation, was typical of the southern region (A-type) and will be illustrated by four ex-

The traditional head scarf, or *tarha*, was usually black among the Fedija, but Kenuzi women preferred different colors: red, green, yellow, or pink.

Decoration of the houses, both inside and outside, was customarily a woman's job. Sometimes a talented woman would be asked to paint all the houses in the village.

amples (Figs. 3, 6, 9, 12) from the settlements of Farriq (Abu Simbel, East Bank) and Qustul near the Sudanese border.

The second (B) type (Figs. 15, 17, 19, 20, 21, 24) was found in northern Kenuzi tribal settlements; our examples are from Dahmit, Kalabsha, and Abu Hor. The main rooms were either barrel vaulted or flat roofed, and the main entrance usually lay in the south wall, that is, perpendicular to the Nile.

The few actual houses that are illustrated here give only an idea of the great variety to be found in Nubian architecture, known primarily for its masterpieces of decorative art. In principle, however, the examples are representative of the usual house plan found in the north and the south of Egyptian Nubia. The houses in middle Nubia are little known, but they seem not to have been greatly different from those in the northern and southern regions.

Southern Nubia

In general, the plan of the "cubiform mud-brick house with flat roof" (A1, A2, A3, A4) had as its basic element an almost square layout with an open, rectangular courtyard as the central communication area. Lines of one-story rooms arranged around it were separated and placed according to their functions.

In the west (or in the east, if the house was located on the river's west bank), facing the river, was a zone of approach with reception hall for visitors and connected to it a guest room, which served as a middle ground between the public and private spheres of the house. Only from this part of the house, which has to be considered as half-public, did windows open onto the street. Here visitors and guests stayed in order to protect the household's privacy and also to protect the family from any possible harm (evil eye!), especially at night.

Along the east side were rooms for storing, cooking, and living, all of which were accessible separately and could be closed off.

Along the south side of the house interior, a lightly roofed area, or loggia, opened onto the courtyard, giving access to the prevailing and cooling north wind. This loggia, together with comparable areas that opened toward the west (A2, A4), served as an open-air living space shaded from the sun, which was also used as a sleeping area during the hot season.

Opposite, that is, usually covering the whole north side of the house (except, see A3) and separated from all the others, lay a group of rooms that formed a compound consisting usually of a courtyard, a large open room known as the *diwani*, or bridal hall, a small storage

and cooking place, and a toilet. This individual compound was the most noteworthy element in the whole house complex and was typical in the south. Accessible by an extra door not visible from the main entrance of the courtyard, the compound was reserved as living quarters either for the young married couple and their children or for the son or daughter about to be married. The small room with cooking facilities was used for storage as well and, during winter months, for sleeping. As there was usually only one toilet per house, the one in this compound was used by the whole family.

As already mentioned, the only real windows of the house were those of the guest room and the entrance hall, which were screened but glassless. In each room, however, were rectangular openings placed high on the walls, vertical slits intended for ventilation only. Light entered the rooms from the doors opened onto the courtyard, doors that were made of wood and equipped with a wooden lock moved by a wooden key (Fig. 1), an old Islamic form of lock.

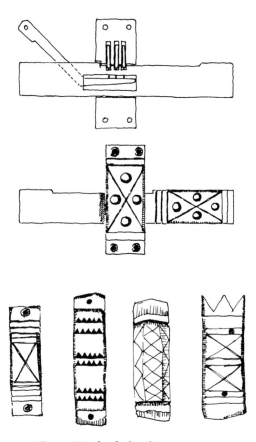

Fig. 1. Wooden locks of Farriq region

51

As long as flat terrain was available, the orthogonal plan described here could be maintained. The right angle dominated as a result of a special method of wall construction. Rather than mud brick or quarry or field stone, a concretelike mixture of gravel, sand, Nile mud, straw, and animal dung—the so-called *tin*—was used as a building material. The *tin* was prepared one or two days ahead and poured into wall forms (boards about half a meter in height, fixed by means of poles on both sides at the width of the desired wall) by the rammed-earth technique. The *tin* had to dry for about two days before the boards could be moved and lifted for the next filling. Thus, to erect all the walls of a house to an average height of 3.5 m took about fifteen days. After the walls were dry, they were plastered on the inside and outside with a mortar of mud and sand. This, as we shall see, was the basic surface upon which decorations were painted.

The flat roofs were constructed with rafters of split palm trunks, which were laid across the tops of finished walls, about one meter apart. They were then covered by mats of palm leaves placed in the opposite direction and finally by a layer of *tin*, which served as good insulation and as protection against occasional heavy rains and high winds. The finished roof lay somewhat lower than the wall tops, since the ends of the rafters, after being well fixed in their position by flat stones, were covered with another section of wall half a meter in height.

While the surface of the courtyard and other unroofed parts of the house was normally left in its natural state of sandy and rocky soil, the floors of the closed rooms and the loggias were of beaten mud covered with a fine sand that was frequently swept and changed. Locally woven reed mats and perhaps a rug, a few tables, some chairs and wooden chests, as well as one or two locally made beds (*angareeb*), sufficed as furniture. Great clay jars were used for storage of food, and water brought up from the Nile was kept and cooled in clay *zirs*, placed in several shady places in the house. Cooking and bread baking was done on round flat plates of iron or clay supported by three legs, or low

Fig. 2. Hearth, built of clay (House A3)

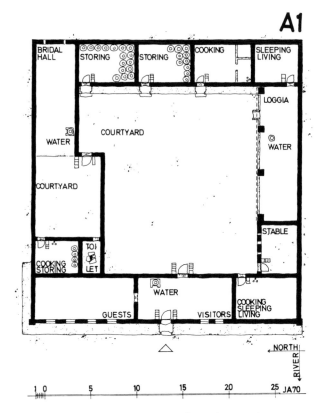

Fig. 3. House A1, Qustul (Scale 1:200)

Fig. 4. General view from northwest (House A1)

cylinders of burnt mud (Fig. 2). This arrangement was found not only in the kitchen but also at any suitable place in other rooms. The presence of several cooking places indicated that several individual family groups were living within the larger clan house.

A1. Our first house example (Fig. 3) was located at the northern edge of Qustul village, built on almost level ground. With its nearly square compound and plain walls about four meters in height, the house gave the impression of a small fortress (Fig. 4).

Proceeding from the entrance hall, one entered the wide courtyard (Fig. 5). Opposite the entrance were two storage rooms and the kitchen. A living-sleeping

Fig. 5. Entrance into courtyard seen from inside (House A1)

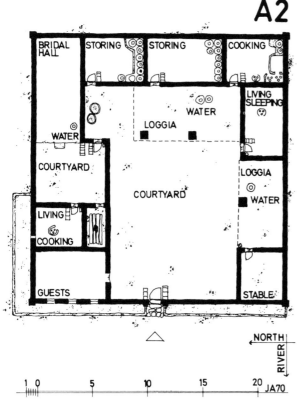

A2

Fig. 6. House A2, Farriq, East Bank (Scale 1:200)

ings, which were more common in northern Nubia. The few decorations were mud-made (cf. Fig. 13). At the back wall of the bridal hall a relief in mud, colored in white and browns, was actually a piece of stylized architecture using crescents, birds, and sword-holding lions as motifs. The tops of the northern and southern walls of the smaller courtyard were crowned by cones of sun-dried Nile mud (cf. Fig. 10). A strip of mud was used decoratively to outline an arch above the door lintels of the kitchen and the storage rooms. The arch provided a place for three china plates to be inset for decoration. A single plate was fixed in the center of the lintel above the gate to the small courtyard. Pilasterlike strips flanking both sides of the main entrance (cf. Figs. 8, 11) and buttresses at the northwest and southwest corners accented the whole façade.

The following three houses (A2, A3, and A4) were located in the area of Farriq (Abu Simbel, East Bank). Although their plans seem to be similar to the one already shown, they will be discussed separately because of differences in detail and situation.

A2. House A2 (Fig. 6) was very reminiscent of the first example. The entrance hall and the room for guests were missing, but the latter simply seems to have been utilized for other purposes, as the windows looking onto the street had been filled in to become merely horizontal slits. On the other hand, the house had two luxurious open-air spaces inside.

The technique of construction and the building materials were similar to those already described. A slight difference is noticeable. Sun-dried mud bricks arranged like a network (Fig. 7) formed the upper edge of the wall of the small courtyard. The lintel part of this en-

Fig. 7. Doorway to bridal courtyard (House A2)

room joined to the south was accessible from a loggia that continued at right angles to the west. A stable for small animals followed. South of the entrance hall, but accessible from the courtyard, was another living-sleeping room with a cooking facility.

The technique of construction and the building materials were like those already described. This house was not painted nor did it contain decorative wall paint-

Fig. 8. Gateway (House A2)

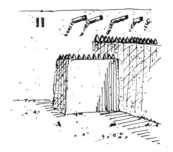

Fig. 10. Toilet in bridal courtyard (House A3)

Fig. 11. Gateway (House A3)

A3

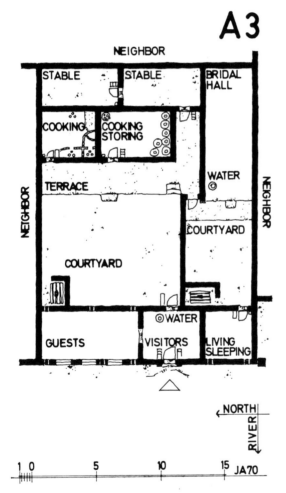

Fig. 9. House A3, Farriq, East Bank (Scale 1:200)

trance was topped with three decorative mud-brick pinnacles (Fig. 7). Similarly, the main gate was surmounted by a construction in mud brick, while pilasterlike strips on both sides extended slightly above the top of the wall (Fig. 8). Its inner side formed an ogee arch, which had stepped outlines and three plates in the center as decoration. The corners of the house were strengthened by buttresses.

A3. Although example A3 (Fig. 9) was situated close to three neighboring buildings, the basic plan was the same, except that the house was somewhat deeper and no sun-protected open-air space was to be found. Construction methods and building materials, as well as the interior installations, were similar to those of examples A1 and A2. A second toilet in the northwest corner of the main courtyard was another differing feature.

With the exception of the western wall of the courtyard, all the walls of the house were painted in light colors. In the same way as in example A1, mud cones adorned the top part of the north wall of the small courtyard and the walls of its unroofed toilet (Fig. 10). Pilasterlike strips flanked the main entrance door and enclosed a framework of bricks set above the lintel in a rhomboid pattern (Fig. 11).

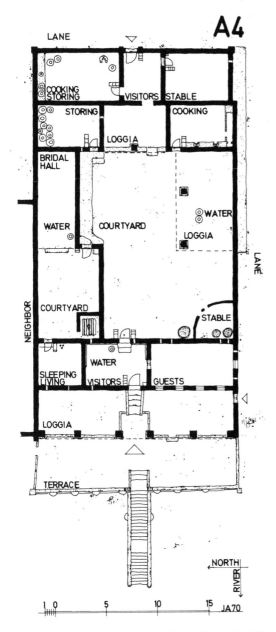

Fig. 12. House A4, Farriq, East Bank (Scale 1:200)

A4. To conclude the description of the southern house type, an example is shown (Fig. 12) that was situated on the river's sloping east bank, at the end of a row of other houses.

A large loggia and an open terrace with a staircase facing the Nile made this house the most attractive one of this group. The riverside entrance has to be considered as the principal approach, and another door

from a side lane was a secondary entrance. Here again, the entrance hall served as a middle ground between the public and private areas. Entering the building from the back, one found a cozy covered sitting place, which led to the main courtyard, a courtyard dominated by an east-west orientated loggia.

Walls, pillars, and roofs were constructed as already noted. Pillars as well as the roughly plastered inner walls of the courtyard were painted in light ochre and all the other walls were painted white.

Other than the painted walls, the house was little decorated. Mud cones adorned the southern wall of the bridal courtyard (cf. Fig. 10), and the lumplike modeled lintel of its entrance had only one plate. Ogee arches were modeled in mud plaster on the walls above the windows of the guest room and were decorated with a single plate in the center. All the doors except the main gate were similarly decorated (Fig. 13). The

Fig. 13. Decorations above doors and windows made of mud plaster (House A4)

main gate was accented by a rectangle, with diagonals above the lintel modeled in an identical way. A simple zigzag frieze ornamented the west façade.

Northern Nubia

From Aswan to Madiq, in the northern part of Nubia where the Kenuzi tribe had settled, a rather different type of house was common. The most obvious difference is the roof, which in some cases was barrel vaulted and in some cases flat, even when the house plans were almost identical (B5a-B5b, B6-B7).

The following examples are houses that were situated between Aswan and Abu Hor, an area south of the First Cataract covering approximately half of the Kenuzi district. The plans did not differ much. The dimensions and the number of rooms depended on either the needs or the wealth of the proprietor, or on the topographical or village situation. Many of the houses seemed to climb up the rocky river banks (B6, B7), but, as far as the terrain allowed, the form remained rectangular.

Usually accessible from village lanes that ran perpendicular to the river, the houses were freestanding, grouped, or connected, with the same north-south orientation. The cell-like rooms for living, sleeping, and cooking were without exception situated in the northern part of the building, opening their doors to the south rather than the north to avoid the cold, continuously blowing north wind during the winter months.

The building of a house started with two basic cells, for living-sleeping and for cooking-storing. Other rooms of the same width and depth could be added later (B4a, B4b). Stables, usually built parallel to the row of rooms, were separated in both construction and decoration. Toilets in houses were not common, as public ones existed in the Kenuzi villages.

A walled courtyard as wide as the row of rooms stretched to the south, where often the main entrance was placed (B5a, B5b, B6, B7). This difference seems worth noting, since, unlike in the southern regions, guest rooms had not been developed in most Kenuzi houses, and strangers still had to be kept out of family life as much as possible. However, benches built near the entrance gates (B3, B6) and the construction of a kind of entrance hall with benches (B2) may have served the purpose of the guest room. Occasionally, a small wall blocked half of the entrance hall, thus obstructing the view of the courtyard from the main entrance (B7 and Fig. 14).

In addition to the entrance hall, another hall was often located in the southern part of the courtyard, which opened to the north and served the family as a sun-protected open-air living space in the summer months (B3, B4b, B5a, B5b, B6, B7). Stables and

Fig. 14. Entrance hall (House B7)

small water huts were found in this area as well. The water hut was a simple construction, usually roofed and open on two sides (B1, B3), or at least one side (B2, B4b, B7), and so placed in the courtyard as to take advantage of prevailing winds to cool the river water stored in the porous clay jars, or *zirs*.

The different functions of the southern courtyard resulted in varying architectural elements that contrasted with the living and cooking cells to the north. The courtyard wall, however, enclosed all the different structures and gave the house a unified outer appearance.

The houses examined will be presented in groups, as there are certain similarities among them. First are three examples (B1, B2, B3), each from different settlements and built on plateaus above the east bank of the Nile. The size of the plateaus certainly must have been the reason for their great extension. In spite of the fact that the settlements were several kilometers apart, the plans of the three houses were nearly identical. All had more than one entrance, but the decorated entrance was considered to be the main gate.

The three houses were built of field stone, mud plastered. Only the decoration surmounting the main entrance and the cornice above the rooms were executed in mud bricks. The flat roofs were built up with the same rammed-earth technique used in southern Nubia.

B1. House B1 (Fig. 15), surveyed in the village of Dahmit (East Bank), had three entrances, a main door in the southwest corner of the courtyard, another door in the eastern wall, and a small door at the northwest corner of the house leading into what could have been a guest room.

The part of the courtyard floor that led from the entrance gate, along the west wall to the front of the

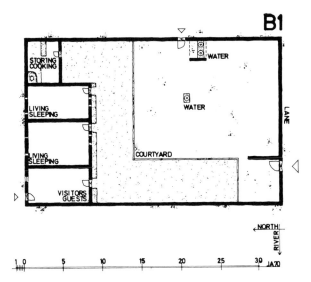

Fig. 15. House B1, Dahmit, East Bank (Scale 1:200)

band separated the white surface of the walls from the soil. Moreover, the gleaming white painted area was covered with colorful stars, flags, palm trees, pigeons, fish, and potted flowers.

B2. A house of Tafa (East Bank) (Fig. 17), somewhat

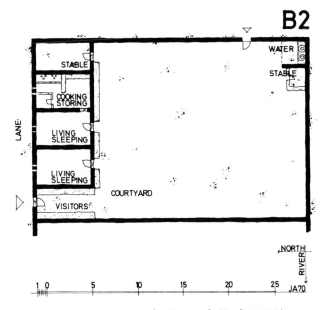

Fig. 17. House B2, Tafa, East Bank (Scale 1:200)

rooms, was smoothly mud plastered, but the ground of the remainder of the courtyard had been left in its natural state.

The kitchen was separated into cooking and storing areas by a step and a cupboardlike balustrade. The two rooms beside the kitchen were probably living-sleeping rooms, whereas the one at the northwest corner may have served as a guest room.

With the exception of the kitchen, the rooms formed one element of architecture and decoration (Fig. 16). The inner walls of the rooms, the walls of the courtyard, and the whole compound on the outside were all painted white. A white, molded cornice terminated the dark-olive painted wall that faced the courtyard. Each door was decorated with three plates set above the lintel and framed by a white painted band, which was continued as a baseboard along the wall; the bench and the plastered zone in front of each of the rooms was painted in a contrasting color. A rust brown baseboard

smaller in size than the one in Dahmit, was entered through a hall meant to be the visitors' area, as it contained mud-plastered benches (*mastabas*) along the walls. Entering the secondary gate at the southeast corner of the courtyard, one passed a water hut and a small stable.

The living quarters consisted of two living-sleeping rooms and a kitchen with a walled-up storage place. A stable ended the row of rooms to the east. Quite unusual for this type of house was the absence of a direct connection between courtyard and kitchen, which could only be entered from the neighboring room.

The most decorative wall was the courtside wall of the living quarters. Painted white and olive, this wall resembled closely the one of house B1. A few ornamental motifs similar to those already mentioned, but rendered only in white and blue, appeared on this wall. A white-blue-white striped band and a molded cornice of mud bricks finished the upper part of the wall. The main portal was decorated with plates and crowned on the outside by an arrangement of pierced semiarches (Fig. 18).

Fig. 16. Doors of individual rooms facing courtyard (House B1)

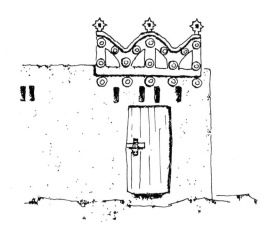

Fig. 18. Main entrance (House B2)

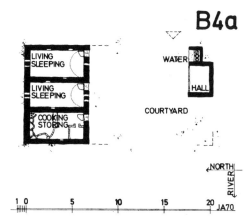

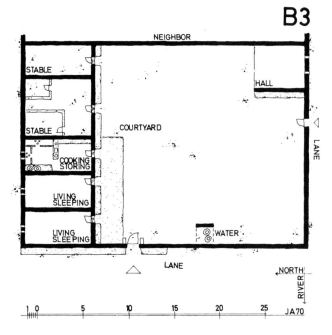

Fig. 19. House B3, Tafa, East Bank (Scale 1:200)

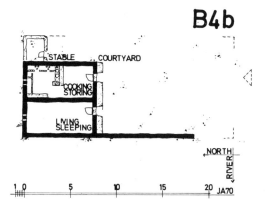

Fig. 20. House B4a, Tafa, East Bank (Scale 1:200); House B4b, Dahmit, East Bank (Scale 1:200)

B3. The third example (Fig. 19) did not differ much in either layout or decoration from the first two houses described. The courtyard lacked a special reception area and was entered by the main entrance in the western wall, which surrounded the compound. Mud-brick benches, or *mastabas*, on both sides of the entrance gate might be considered as a substitute for the reception area. The house's second entrance led to the courtyard, in the southeast corner of which was a flat-roofed open hall.

DEVELOPMENT OF TYPE B

Two plans (Fig. 20) will demonstrate how a house of the Kenuzi type developed. Both examples, one with a flat roof and one with a barrel-vaulted roof, demonstrate the initial stage of the building process.

B4a. One compound at Tafa (East Bank) consisted only of the two basic rooms, for living-sleeping and cooking-storing. As the outer wall of the kitchen facing east was not plastered, and the stable was added rather roughly in field stone, one may suppose a future extension of the house in that direction. A boundary to the west had been established in the already plastered western wall of the courtyard. The location of the southwest corner of the house, however, was still not evident.

B4b. The two barrel-vaulted rooms and the flat-roofed kitchen seen in an example at Dahmit (East Bank) have to be considered, also, as a partly finished structure.

Doors of Nubian houses were sometimes painted in abstract designs, chosen and executed by the owner himself.

The dark mud-brick wall provided a background upon which fantasies of design were executed with paint brush and knife. Here elaborate outdoor gates opened onto a large courtyard. An inner door of similar design contributed to the sense of space and color that Nubian architects developed in their houses.

Familiar objects, often depicted on house walls and doors, were elaborate and fantastic, such as this wheeled impression of the Sudan Railways' steamboat.

House interiors varied. In most Fedija houses, only the *diwani*, or bridal hall, was decorated with rows of colorful plates woven of palm fiber. In other parts of the house, simple mud relief and a band of paint were used to outline areas in rooms or to decorate the storage jars.

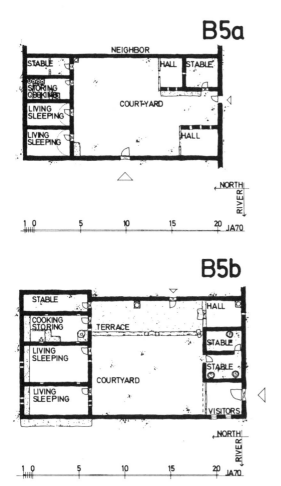

B5a

STABLE | NEIGHBOR | HALL | STABLE
STORING COOKING | COURT-YARD
LIVING SLEEPING
LIVING SLEEPING | HALL

NORTH
RIVER

1 0   5   10   15   20   JA70

B5b

STABLE | HALL
COOKING STORING | TERRACE
LIVING SLEEPING | STABLE
COURTYARD | STABLE
LIVING SLEEPING | VISITORS

NORTH
RIVER

1 0   5   10   15   20   JA70

Fig. 21. House B5a, Kalabsha, East Bank (Scale 1:200);
House B5b, Abu Hor (Scale 1:200)

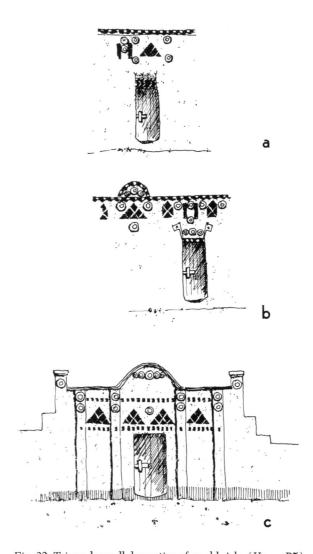

Fig. 22. Triangular wall decoration of mud bricks (House B5)

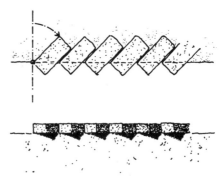

Fig. 23. Molded cornice of mud brick
(House B5)

Further extension could be imagined to the west, for instance, with the addition of a stable to the kitchen area. The eastern and southern boundaries seem to have been already defined by the hall and the water hut.

The main entrances of both partly completed houses might have been located in either the eastern or the western wall of the courtyard.

Two further plans (Fig. 21), although smaller in size than the first three, are almost identical in basic plan if one does not consider the additions in the southern part of the courtyard.

B5a, B5b. These two houses, located in villages close to each other—Kalabsha (East Bank) (B5a and Fig. 22b, c) and Abu Hor (B5b and Fig. 22a)—had certain details in common, such as an olive-colored wall on the rooms facing the courtyard, a wall finished by a pronged

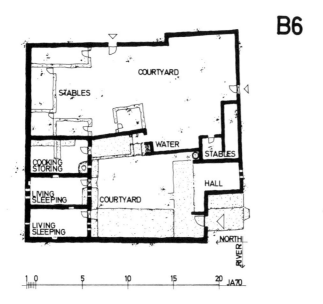

B6

Fig. 25. Gateway (House B7)

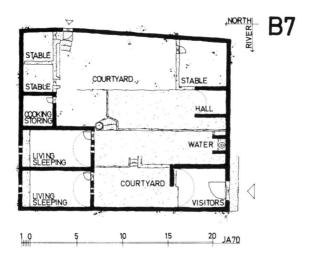

B7

Fig. 24. House B6, Dahmit, East Bank (Scale 1:300);
House B7, Dahmit, East Bank (Scale 1:200)

molded cornice of mud bricks (Fig. 23); and a decorative element, a variation of the usual vertical slits, which seemed to perforate the wall for ventilation purposes (Fig. 22a, *b*). But this network of mud bricks forming a triangular pattern was actually a blind brickwork, and the same pattern reappeared on the wall above the main entrance of house B5a (Fig. 22c).

The rooms of house B5a, surprisingly, were much smaller than the others described here, but this was apparently not due to the limitations of the barrel-vaulted construction.

B6, B7. The two final examples (Fig. 24) from Dahmit (East Bank) were not greatly different from those already described, except that their irregular and terraced arrangement was made necessary by the topography of the river bank on which they were built. Staircases and balustrades ran parallel to the slope and the halls, stables, and water huts were of different sizes, especially in the southern part of the courtyard (Fig. 25). Although the differences in level created a sense of disunity in the secondary rooms, the primary living units were hardly affected.

PLATES

1. Egyptian Nubia began south of the First Cataract of the Nile, shown in its rocky outcroppings at the port of Aswan.

2. The post boat of the Sudan Railways was the principal motorized means of communication between the Nubian villages located on the more than two hundred miles of riverbank between Aswan, Egypt, and Wadi Halfa, in the Sudan. The boat brought supplies and money orders from fathers and husbands working in faraway cities.

3. Local transportation and freight were handled by graceful lateen-sailed feluccas.

4. In a land filled with the monuments of past civilizations—Pharaonic, Byzantine, and Greek—the Nubians built their houses and tilled their fields.

5. For the Nubians, the monuments were part of their daily lives; the giant pillars and statuary sometimes provided shade for the shepherds.

Storage containers ornamented with shells were hung from the ceiling of the *diwani*, or bridal hall, of most Fedija houses.

In Kenuzi houses, the interior became an elaborate montage, in which all elements available to the Nubian villager were utilized in a mosaic of color and texture.

6. On the day of a Nubian marriage, the groom was danced to his bride in a formal procession, the *seefa*, headed by drummers, singers, and the village chanter, or "forever" man.

7. All the villagers followed in the procession, singing wedding songs and responding to the impromptu verses of the "forever" man, recited in praise of the nuptial couple's ancestors. An old lady close to the bride's family carried some of the groom's presents to his bride.

8. Before the official *ma'zoun*, the groom read the wedding verses from the Quran and formally stated his desire to marry.

9. The bride also read the Quran before the *ma'zoun* and gave her consent to the marriage.

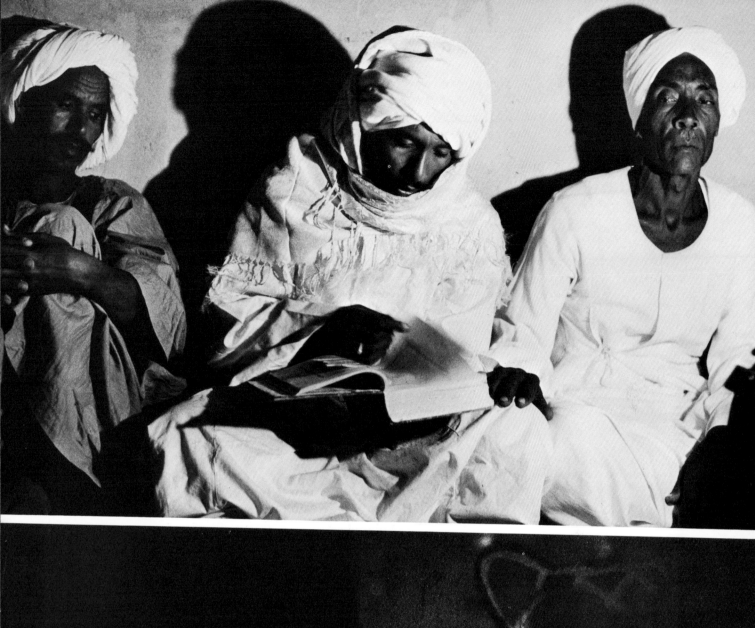
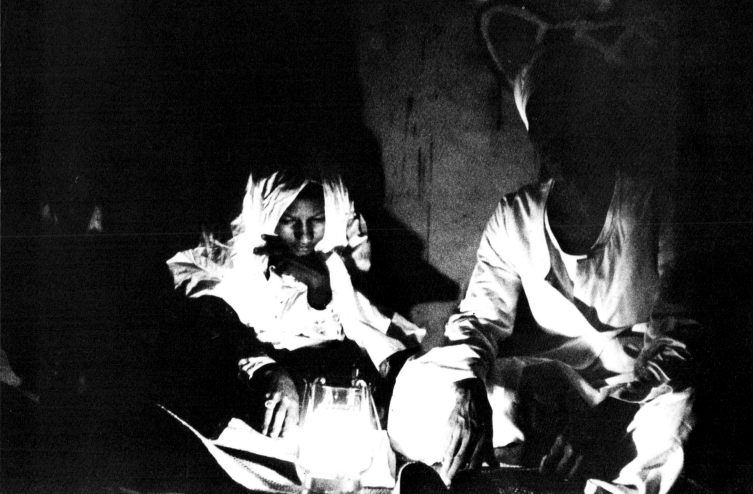

10. When the formalities were completed, the *ma‘zoun* prepared the *gofad*, the painted wooden receptacle in the foreground. The *gofad* was filled with a paste of perfumed henna, which was offered to each of the wedding guests for good luck.

11. The ceremony of the bestowal of wealth took place as each of the groom's close relatives presented a gift of money or shares in land, houses, cows, or water wheels. While the groom received gifts from his male friends and relatives, the bride was receiving similar gifts of jewelry from her mother, aunts, and other female relatives. This ceremony essentially established the dowry of the young couple and determined whether or not they would be able to stay in the village and subsist on traditional agriculture, or whether the new groom must migrate to the city to support his new family. The *ma‘zoun* also certified the marriage contract at this time.

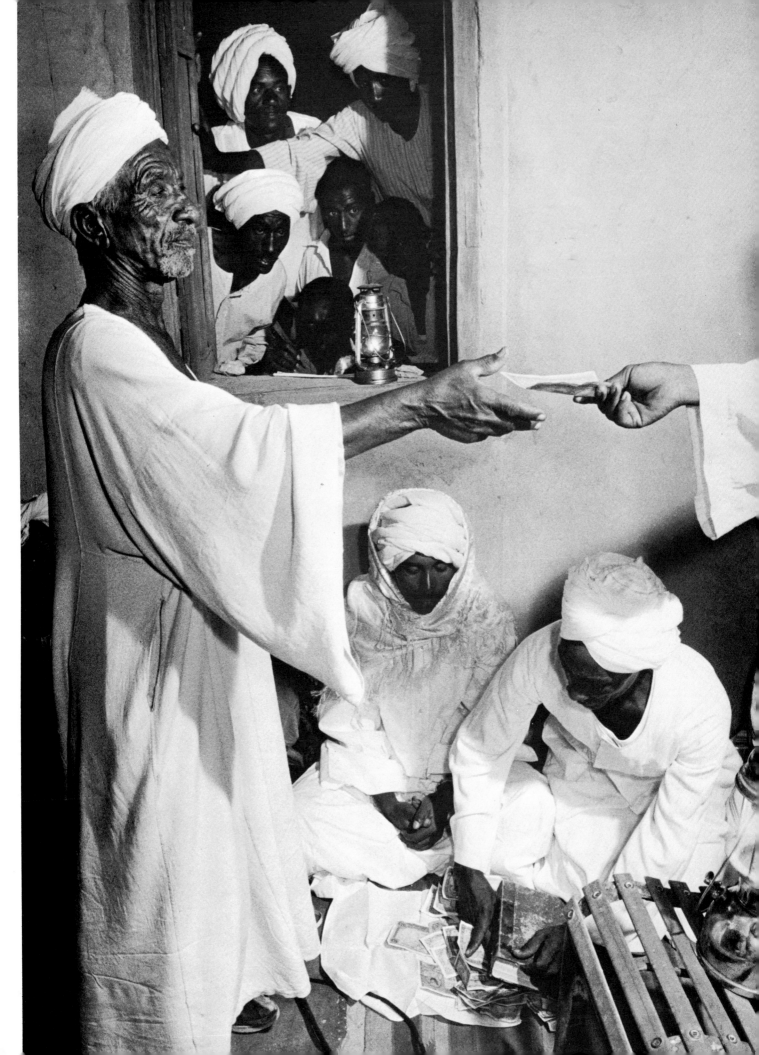

12. The mother of the groom prepared the plates of traditional dates and popcorn which would be offered to the women of the village when they came to present *karray*, or exchange gifts.

13. Women of the village enjoyed the popcorn and dates while they waited in the courtyard of the groom's house to offer traditional small gifts to his mother.

14. Father of the groom.

15. Every inch of the scarce arable land along the banks of the Nile was utilized,
and the land was divided into plots by means of low earthen walls, *fah*, which
held the irrigation water on the land and also served as boundary lines for owners.

16. Nile water was lifted onto the land by means of the water wheel, or *eskalay*.
Two *eskalays* in operation are at right; the water wheel at left is being constructed.

17. Cows pushed the wheel of the *eskalay*, thus lifting an endless cycle of buckets filled with water up onto the land.

18. Another, much less efficient irrigation device was the hand-operated shadoof, *keeyay*, used to irrigate the lowlands near the river.

20. Cultivating was also a cooperative process. In late afternoon and evening, a group of men, usually kinsmen, would work together on commonly owned land. Each family in turn provided tea or refreshment for the men after the work period.

19. By day, a man worked his own land, sowing the seed and turning over the soil.

21. *Kashrangegg*, a quick-growing type of fodder, was harvested two or three times each season to be fed to the animals. Animal husbandry was an important source of cash income, especially in the Kenuzi area, where agricultural land was limited and covered by water during most of the year.

22. To supplement the products of cultivation, women had to search for camel's-thorn and other shrubs to feed the animals.

23. Millet (*dhourra*) was
the principal grain
grown in Nubia in recent
years, although many of
the seeds were eaten
by small birds before
they could be harvested.
Dhourra stalks were
stored on the roofs of
the houses and fed to
the animals in winter.

24. During harvest,
men threshed the grain
with the fronds of palm
trees, and then the
women tossed the millet
on woven reed plates,
to separate the grain
from the chaff.

25. Boys took the grain on donkeyback to the mill, where it was ground into flour. Until recently, the grain was ground by hand in a stone mill.

26. Flour, water, and salt were ingredients in *shayleeya*, a kind of fine spaghetti like breakfast cereal.

27. Dates were an important source of wealth and prestige in southern Egyptian Nubia and the Sudan.

28. Many people owned shares in each palm tree, and the produce was divided annually at the time of harvest.

29. Dates as well as grain were stored in large clay pots, *goosay*, often painted and decorated in designs similar to those on the walls of the houses and on the interior walls of the courtyards.

30. Every product of the date palm was utilized. Dried dead fronds were used for fuel and the fibers made into rope.

31. Bundles of date palm fiber were tied together to make ceilings and walls for animal shelters.

32. Date palm fibers were also used for brooms, scouring pads, and bandages. The fibers were dyed and woven into plates, bowls, and mats to cover the floors of the houses.

33. The weaving of reed plates from the palm fibers was a skill passed on from mother to daughter.

34. In leisure hours women plaited each other's hair into tiny braids.

35. Sometimes gold and silver coins were woven into the braids of hair. Coins were used in this way only in the Kenuzi area recently, but the practice was formerly common throughout Nubia.

36. Jewelry in gold and silver and semi-precious stones was passed on from mother to daughter at the time of the girl's marriage and became the personal property of the bride. The pendant pictured here, of an older design, is in silver, turquoise, lapislazuli, topaz, and carnelian. Amber and coral were also popular, as well as necklaces of polished agate.

37. The groom also offered gifts of jewelry to his bride, such as these rings and bracelets of silver.

39. Nubian houses were remarkable reflections of the tastes and interests of their owners. The Fedija houses of southern Nubia were built around a large central open courtyard. Loggias and spacious rooms surrounding the court were well designed for both winter and summer climates.

38. The jewelry worn by the young married woman signified that she had reached the age of adulthood and responsibility in a Nubian community.

40. Nubian house designers may have been influenced by the presence of Pharaonic antiquities around them. The temple pillars of Dendur are echoed in the pillars of the Nubian houses above, on the hillside.

41. Kenuzi homeowners had to adjust to different topographical situations as they were forced progressively by Nile waters to move their houses farther and farther away from the flat plateaus on the banks to the stony hills near the mountains. In this Kenuzi village, several of the barrel-vaulted roofs are visible. Executed entirely in mud brick, the barrel vault was a distinctive difference between Kenuzi and Fedija architecture.

42. This Kenuzi house used the steep slope to advantage, creating a decorative staircase from the river to the main door of the house. Painting and decoration of the walls, both inside and outside, was more elaborate among the Kenuz. Façades and gates were often ornamented with mud relief, and lintel, pillars, and doors were topped with mud-brick embellishments.

43. Kenuzi homes also appeared as row houses, to utilize all available space.

44. Houses were replastered frequently, for both utility and beauty. The replastering was a neighborhood enterprise, and, when completed, provided a new surface upon which the village artists could paint and decorate.

45. Boys at play would often race along the *mastabas*, or benches of smoothly plastered mud built along the fronts of the houses. Here neighbors and friends of the family gathered in the evening to talk and enjoy the view of the river. The design on the face of this house is cut out in mud and whitewashed. Such work might have been done by the owner of the house, or by talented neighbors.

46. Boys played the jumping game of *warjay*, which is pictured in Pharaonic wall paintings.

47. Tracing designs in the sand was a pastime for both boys and girls, and *kallay*, a kind of chess, was played with knuckle bones, stones, or dried balls of dung as pieces. Children played the game, using nine holes in the sand.

48. Men often played a more complicated version of *kallay*, using twenty-five holes in the sand.

49. Children swam early in Nubia.

The barrel-vaulted roofed hall in Kenuzi houses was more simply decorated than the interior rooms.

Pillars and other embellishments executed in mud were often part of the painted façades of the houses.

Bands of design were sometimes painted over the entire façade of the house.

Openwork and relief in mud brick, painted in white on a dark background, gave a pleasant harmony to the houses.

50. Boys made their own toy sailboats from wood or tin or even baked mud and tried to launch them in the Nile, long before they were taught to help sail the feluccas.

51. Familiar objects used in daily life were painted on house walls.

52. Painted on a wall of this house is a depiction of the holy Muslim city of Mecca, with the sacred *ka^{c}ba* in the center.

53. Two feluccas and their owners' names are painted on this house wall.

54. People from all sections of Nubia traveled to the Kenuzi villages to attend the *moulids*, or saint's day celebrations. Boatloads of men, women, and children from up and down the Nile would arrive in the early morning of the day of the *moulid*.

55. Fathers and sons arriving at the *moulid* would head for the mosque.

56. The shrine of the saint to be honored was visited next.

57. After the religious ceremony of the *moulid* came the dancing, *kaff*, by the men, to music of the great skin drums.

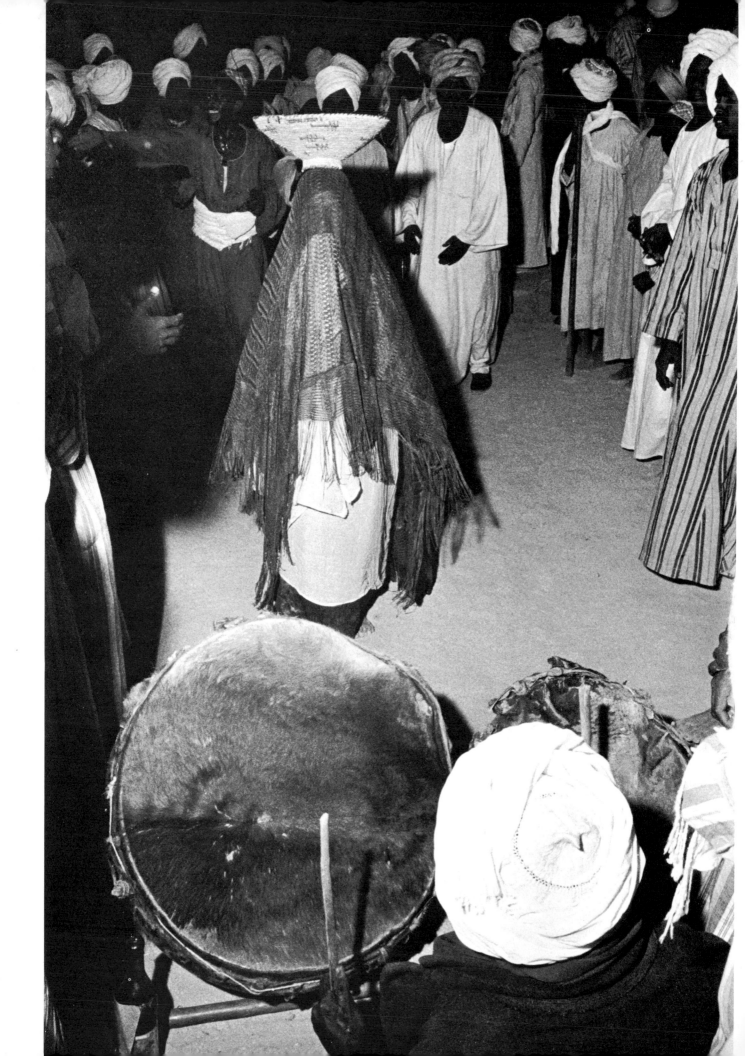

59. Then came the feast, to which all members of the Kenuzi tribe who were hosts at the *moulid* contributed. Bread and trays of dates and popcorn were offered by each lineage of the tribe, as well as the traditional meat, usually that of a sheep, slaughtered ceremonially earlier in the day.

58. Women also danced, usually veiled, with an offering of sugar or grain on their heads, promised to the saint in fulfillment of a vow, *nadr*.

60. Trays of dates and popcorn were covered with woven reed plates until the beginning of the feast.

61. Children sometimes organized their own *moulids*, in imitation of their parents. Here two small girls dance, veiled, like their mothers.

62. Small boys singing at a children's *moulid*.

63. Children building their own shrine.

64. The mourning ceremony after death (*taffer*) was an occasion, like the marriage and the *moulid*, when the entire community was expected to assemble to support the bereaved. In this photo, a death has just occurred in the village and all the people are hurrying up the bank to offer condolences.

65. Fedija graveyards were situated in the sandy areas behind the villages, close to the mountains. Before the woman's grave in the foreground a bowl had been placed, where offerings of water were brought on feast days by relatives of the dead person.

66. Kenuzi graves were terraced rock mounds utilizing the materials of the barren countryside.

The ornamentation of this entryway was entirely composed of mud and mud brick, cut out and then painted.

Today even the tops of the palm trees are covered by the waters of the Nile.

67. Nubians speak of their native land as *balad el-aman,* "land of safety," where people were secure and at peace, and men were free to ride through the palm groves.

68. Men could relax after a day's work.

69. Women could enjoy the security of their friends and families.

70. Fish, which could be eaten at home or sold in Aswan, were still another resource of Nubia, although not all Nubians ate fish.

71. Without the support of migrant kinsmen many communities could not have existed. Thus, some villages consisted principally of women whose husbands, sons, and fathers worked in the cities of Egypt and the Sudan to supplement family incomes.

72. With the beginning of the Aswan High Dam, all the villages of Nubia were threatened. The Egyptian government made plans for resettling the Nubians north of Aswan, near Kom Ombo.

73. The prospect of leaving their ancestral villages and moving to a strange region created great anxiety in the Nubian community.

74. The old people in particular were fearful of what the move might bring.

75. Moving was a difficult process, despite the help of Egyptian government officials assigned to ease the situation.

76. Animals also were moved.

77. The Egyptian government offered plots of land and constructed new houses in Kom Ombo to recompense the Nubians for their loss. But the small stone structures bore little resemblance to the spacious homes along the Nile in Old Nubia.

79. In the newly plastered houses, the customary china plates could be inserted above the doors. Courtyards were half roofed and *mastabas* were built along outer walls. By rearranging and adding rooms, some Nubians were able to create in the smaller units a greater sense of comfort and space.

78. Undismayed, many Nubians immediately began to remodel their new houses, first by plastering the rough stone to create a smooth surface for traditional wall paintings and decoration.

80. The old land has disappeared now, flooded completely
by the waters of Lake Nasser. The dunes and the rocks are gone,
and the villages.

81. The migratory birds that flocked and rested along this section of the Nile pass quickly over it now, for little greenery is left.

82. The palm trees lie under water with the houses and the monuments of ancient civilizations. But the traditional culture, which produced the villages of a proud people, has not been obliterated; it continues to live and find fresh expression in the settlements of New Nubia at Kom Ombo.

SELECTED BIBLIOGRAPHY

Abdalla, Ismaᶜil Hussein. 1967. "Historical studies on the transfer and resettlement of the Halfa population at Khashm el Girba." M.A. thesis, Sudan Research Unit, University of Khartoum.

———. 1970. "The choice of Khashm el Girba area for the resettlement of the Halfawis." *Sudan Notes and Records* 51:56–74.

Abdel Rahman, El Amin. 1969. "Factors in the adjustment of Khashm-el Girba tenants to a new location and new type of agriculture." Ph.D. dissertation, Cornell University.

Abdel Rahman, Mohamed. 1964. "Town on the move: 50,000 people start a new life in the Sudan." *Shell Magazine* 44(695):378–383.

Abdel Rassoul, Kawthar. 1966. "Economic activities of the Sayidis in Egyptian Nubia." In *Contemporary Egyptian Nubia*, edited by Robert A. Fernea, II, 340–351. New Haven: Human Relations Area Files, Inc.

———.1967. "Space relations and tribal formation in Korosko (Egyptian Nubia)." *Wiener Völkerkündliche Mitteilungen*.

Adams, William Y. 1964. "Post-pharaonic Nubia in the light of archaeology, I." *Journal of Egyptian Archaeology* 50:102–120.

———. 1965. "Post-pharaonic Nubia in the light of archaeology, II." *Journal of Egyptian Archaeology* 51:160–178.

———. 1966. "Post-pharaonic Nubia in the light of archaeology, III." *Journal of Egyptian Archaeology* 52: 147–162.

———. 1967. "Continuity and change in Nubian cultural history." *Sudan Notes and Records* 48:1–32.

———. 1968. "Settlement pattern in microcosm: The changing aspect of a Nubian village during twelve centuries." In *Settlement Archaeology*, edited by Kwangchih Chang, pp. 174–207. Palo Alto: National Press Books.

Ayyoub, Abd El-Rahman. 1968. *The verbal system in a dialect of Nubian: Being a description of the verbal function in the structures called "relatio" and "relation adjunct" as spoken in the Halfa district*. Linguistic Monograph Series, no. 2, Sudan Research Unit, University of Khartoum.

Bell, Herman. 1968. "The tone system of Mahas Nubian." *Journal of American Languages* 7(1):26–32.

———. 1970. *Place names in the belly of stones*. Linguistics Monograph Series, no. 5, Sudan Research Unit, University of Khartoum.

Blackenburg, Peter, and Klemens Hubert. 1969. *The Khashm el-Girba settlement scheme in Sudan: An appraisal for the World Food Program*. Berlin: Institut für ausländische Wirtschaft der technischen Universität.

Burkhardt, John L. 1819. *Travels in Nubia*. London: John Murray.

Callender, Charles. 1966. "The Mehannab: A Kenuz tribe." In *Contemporary Egyptian Nubia*, edited by Robert A. Fernea, II, 183–217. New Haven: Human Relations Area Files, Inc.

———, and Fadwa el Guindi. 1971. *Life crisis rituals among the Kenuz*. Case Western Reserve University Studies in Anthropology, no. 3. Cleveland.

Cavendish, M. W. 1966. "The custom of placing pebbles on Nubian graves." *Sudan Notes and Records* 17:151–156.

Dzierzykray-Rogalski, Tadensz, and Elizabeth Prominska. 1968. "The influence of ecological factors upon the mortality structure of the inhabitants in the Wadi Halfa region (Sudan)." *African Bulletin* 8:41–56.

El Adly, Farouk M. 1969. "The local communities of new Nubia: The effects of migration and resettlement with special reference to family organization in Sayala village." Ph.D. dissertation, University of Cairo.

El Guindi, Fadwa. 1966. "Ritual and the river in Dahmit." In *Contemporary Egyptian Nubia*, edited by Robert A. Fernea, II, 239–256. New Haven: Human Relations Area Files, Inc.

El Katsha, Samiha. 1969. "The impact of environmental change on the marriage institution: The case of Kanuba settlers." M.A. thesis, American University in Cairo.

El Sawi, Shahira. 1965. "The Nubian woman in Cairo: Patterns of adjustment; a case study of five families." M.A. thesis, American University in Cairo.

El-Zein, Abdel Hamid. 1966*a*. "Socio-economic implications of the water wheel in Adendan, Nubia." In *Contemporary Egyptian Nubia*, edited by Robert A. Fernea, II, 298–322. New Haven: Human Relations Area Files, Inc.

———. 1966*b*. "Water and wheel in a Nubian village." M.A. thesis, American University in Cairo.

Emery, Walter. 1965. *Lost land emerging*. New York: Charles Schribner's Sons.

Fahim, Hussein M. 1966. "Change in rituals in Kanuba: Salat El-Guma and El-Zikr." M.A. thesis, American University in Cairo.

———. 1968. "The resettlement of Egyptian Nubians: A case study in development and change." Ph.D. dissertation, University of California at Berkeley.

———. 1972. *Nubian resettlement in the Sudan*. Miami: Field Research Projects.

Fathi, Hassan. 1966. "Notes on Nubian architecture." In *Contemporary Egyptian Nubia*, edited by Robert A. Fernea, I, 72–76. New Haven: Human Relations Area Files, Inc.

Fernea, Elizabeth Warnock. 1970. *A view of the Nile*. New York: Doubleday.

Fernea, Robert A. 1963. "The ethnological survey of Egyptian Nubia: A progress report." *Current Anthropology* 4:1.

———, ed. 1966*a*. *Contemporary Egyptian Nubia*. 2 vols. New Haven: Human Relations Area Files, Inc.

———. 1966*b*. "Integrating factors in a non-corporate community." In *Contemporary Egyptian Nubia*, edited by Robert A. Fernea, II, 260–287. New Haven: Human Relations Area Files, Inc.

———. 1970. "Nubian migration: A cultural phenomenon." In *VIIme congrès international des sciences, anthropologiques et ethnologiques, Moscou*, IX, 236–243.

———, and John G. Kennedy. 1966. "Initial adaptations to resettlement: A new life for Egyptian Nubians." *Current Anthropology* 7:349–354.

Gadallah, Fawzi A. 1959. "The Egyptian contribution to Nubian Christianity." *Sudan Notes and Records* 40: 38–43.

Geiser, Peter. 1966. "Some impressions concerning the nature and extent of stabilization and urbanization in Nubian society." In *Contemporary Egyptian Nubia*, edited by Robert A. Fernea, I, 143–169. New Haven: Human Relations Area Files, Inc.

———. 1967. "Some differential factors affecting population movement: The Nubian case." *Human Organization* 26(3):164–177.

Gerster, Georg. 1964. *Nubien—Goldland am Nil*. Zurich and Stuttgart: Artemis Verlag.

Griffiths, J. Gwyn. 1955. "Bilingualism among the Mahass." *Man* 55(164):154–155.

Haikal, Bahiga. 1966. "Residence patterns in Ismailia, Ballana." In *Contemporary Egyptian Nubia*, edited by Robert A. Fernea, II, 289–298. New Haven: Human Relations Area Files, Inc.

Hair, P. E. H. 1964. "Christianity in medieval Nubia and the Sudan: A bibliographical note." *Bulletin of the Society for African Church History* 1(3–4):67–73.

Hassan, Dafalla. 1965. "Notes on the history of Wadi-Halfa town." *Sudan Notes and Records* 46:8–26.

Herzog, Rolf. 1957. *Die Nubier*. Deutsche Akademie der Wissenschaften zu Berlin, Völkerkündliche Forschungen, Band 2. Berlin.

Hillelson, S. 1930. "Nubian origins." *Sudan Notes and Records* 13:137–148.

Horton, Alan W. 1964. *The Egyptian Nubians: Some information on their ethnography and resettlement*. American Universities Field Staff Reports Service, Northeast Africa Series, vol. XI, no. 2. Hanover, N.H.

Jungfleisch, Marcel. 1946. "Hasan Suliman Kashif, of Nubia." *Sudan Notes and Records* 28:239–240.

Kennedy, John G. 1966. "Occupational adjustment in a previously resettled Nubian village." In *Contemporary Egyptian Nubia*, edited by Robert A. Fernea, II, 355–373. New Haven: Human Relations Area Files, Inc.

———. 1967*a*. "Mushahra: A Nubian concept of supernatural danger and theory of taboo." *American Anthropologist* 69(6):685–702.

———. 1967*b*. "Nubian *zar* ceremonies as psychotherapy." *Human Organization* 26(4):185–194.

———. 1970*a*. "Circumcision and excision in Egyptian Nubia." *Man* n.s. 5(2):175–191.

———. 1970*b*. "Aman Doger: Nubian monster of the Nile." *Journal of American Folklore* 83(330):438–445.

Kirwan, L. P. 1937. "A survey of Nubian origins." *Sudan Notes and Records* 20:47–62.

———. 1961. "Nubia's Christian age." *Unesco Courier* 14:38–39.

———. 1963. "Land of Abu Simbel." *Geographical Journal* 129(3):261–273.

Klevel, J. G. 1964*a*. "The housing situation in Wadi Halfa town and rural areas." *Sudan Economic and Financial Review*. Special issue, no. 3.

———. 1964*b*. "Some aspects of emigration from Wadi Halfa rural area in Sudan." *Sudan Economic and Financial Review*. Special issue, no. 3.

Kronenberg, A., and W. Kronenberg. 1963. "Preliminary report on anthropological field work in Sudanese Nubia, 1961–1962." *Kush* 11:302–311.

———. 1964. "Preliminary report on anthropological field work in Sudanese Nubia, 1962–1963." *Kush* 12:282–290.

———. 1965*a*. "Preliminary report on the anthropological field work in Sudanese Nubia, 1964." *Kush* 13:205–212.

———. 1965*b*. "Parallel cousin: Marriage in medieval and modern Nubia." *Kush* 13:241–260.

Lee, David R. 1969*a*. "The Nubian house: Persistence of a cultural tradition." *Landscape* 18(1):36–39.

———. 1969*b*. "Factors influencing choice of house-type: A geographic analysis from the Sudan." *The Professional Geographer* 21: 393–397.

Macgaffey, Wyatt. 1961. "The history of Negro migrations in the northern Sudan." *Southwestern Journal of Anthropology* 17(2):178–197.

MacMichael, Harold A. 1922. *A history of the Arabs in the Sudan*. London: Cambridge University Press.

Marks, Anthony, Joel Scheneir, and T. R. Hays. 1968. "Survey and excavations in the Dongola reach (Sudan)." *Current Anthropology* 9(4):319–323.

Michalowski, Kazimierz. 1966. *Faras, centre artistique de la Nubie Chrétienne*. Leiden: Netherlands Instituut voor het Nabije Oosten, Scholae Adriani de Buck Memoriae.

———. 1967. *Faras, die Kathedrale aus de Wüstensand*. Zurich and Cologne: Benziger Verlag.

———. 1970. "Open problems of Nubian art in the light of the discoveries at Faras." In *Kunst und Geschichte Nubiens in Christlicher Zeit*, edited by E. Dinkler, pp. 11–28. Recklinghausen: Aurel Bongers Verlag.

Millet, Nicholas. 1964. "Some notes on the linguistic background of modern Nubian." In *Contemporary Egyptian Nubia*, edited by Robert A. Fernea, I, 59–71. New Haven: Human Relations Area Files, Inc.

———. 1968. "Meroitic Nubia." Ph.D. dissertation, Yale University.

Monneret de Villard, Ugo. 1935. *La Nubia medioevale*, vols. I-II. Cairo: Imprimerie de l'Institut Français d'Archéologie Orientale.

———. 1938. *Storia della Nubia Cristiana*. Orientalia Christiana Analecta 118. Rome: Pontificio Institutum Orientalium Studiorum.

———. 1957. *La Nubia medioevale*, vols. III-IV. Cairo: Imprimerie de l'Institut Français d'Archéologie Orientale.

Musad, Mustafa M. 1959. "The downfall of the Christian Nubian kingdoms." *Sudan Notes and Records* 40:124–128.

———. 1967. "Islam in medieval Nubia." In *Nubie*, pp. 165–176. Cahiers d'Histoire Egyptienne, vol. X. Cairo.

Nadim, Nawal El Messiri. 1965. "The sheikh cult in Dahmit life." M.A. thesis, American University in Cairo.

———. 1966. "The sheikh cult in Dahmit life." In *Contemporary Egyptian Nubia*, edited by Robert A. Fernea, II, 219–237. New Haven: Human Relations Area Files, Inc.

Reisner, George A. 1910. *The Nubian archaeological survey report for 1907–1908*, vol. I. Cairo: National Printing Department.

Riad, Mohamed. 1962. "Sayala: A contribution to the study of Nubian ecology." *Faculty of Arts Bulletin* (University of Ain Shams in Cairo).

———. 1963. "Korosko." *Faculty of Arts Bulletin* (University of Ain Shams in Cairo).

———. 1966. "Patterns of Ababda economy in Egyptian Nubia." In *Contemporary Egyptian Nubia*, edited by Robert A. Fernea, II, 325–339. New Haven: Human Relations Area Files, Inc.

St. John, James August. 1834. *Egypt and Mohammed Ali, or Travels in the Valley of the Nile*, vol. I. London.

Scudder, Thayer. 1966*a*. "The economic basis of Egyptian Nubian labour migration." In *Contemporary Egyptian Nubia*, edited by Robert A. Fernea, I, 100–142. New Haven: Human Relations Area Files, Inc.

———. 1966*b*. "Man-made lakes and social change." *Engineering and Science* 29:18–22.

Shaw, D. J. 1967. "Resettlement from the Nile in Sudan." *Middle East Journal* 21(2):462–487.

Shinnie, P. L. 1954. *Medieval Nubia*. Sudan Antiquities Service Museum Pamphlet, no. 2. Khartoum.

———. 1965. "New light on medieval Nubia." *Journal of African History* 6(3):263–273.

———. 1967. *Meroe*. New York: Frederick Praeger.

———. 1971. "The culture of medieval Nubia and its impact on Africa." In *Sudan in Africa*, edited by Y. F. Hasan, pp. 42–50. Sudan Research Unit, University of Khartoum.

Shukairy, Najwa. 1966. "A study of obligations on death occasions among Cairo migrants from a southern Nubian village." In *Contemporary Egyptian Nubia*, edited by Robert A. Fernea, I, 170–177. New Haven: Human Relations Area Files, Inc.

Sid Ahmed, Galal El Din. 1968. "Marketing of agricultural products of Khashm el Girba." M.Sc. thesis, University of Khartoum.

Sorbo, Gunnar. 1971. *Economic adaptations in Khashm el Girba: A study of settlement problems in the Sudan*. Sudan Research Unit, University of Khartoum.

Trigger, Bruce. 1964. "Merotic and Eastern Sudanic: A linguistic relationship?" *Kush* 12:188–194.

———. 1965. *History and settlement in lower Nubia*. Yale University Publications in Anthropology, no. 69. New Haven.

———. 1966. "New light on the history of settlement in lower Nubia." In *Contemporary Egyptian Nubia*, edited by Robert A. Fernea, I, 21–58. New Haven: Human Relations Area Files, Inc.

———. 1968. "New light on the history of lower Nubia." *Anthropologica* 10:81–106.

———. 1969a. "The myth of Meroe and the African Iron Age." *African Historical Studies* 2(1):23–50.

———. 1969b. "The personality of the Sudan." In *Eastern African History*, edited by D. F. McCall, N. R. Bennett, and J. Butler, III, 74–99. New York: Praeger.

———. 1970. "The cultural ecology of Christian Nubia." In *Kunst und Geschichte Nubiens in Christlicher Zeit*, edited by E. Dinkler, pp. 347–386. Recklinghausen: Aurel Bongers Verlag.

Vercoutter, J. 1961. "Sudanese Nubia and African history." *United Nations Review* 8:23.

Wendorf, Fred, ed. 1968. *The prehistory of Nubia*. 2 vols. Dallas: Southern Methodist University Press.

Wenzel, Marian. 1972. *House decoration in Nubia*. London: Gerald Duckworth.

INDEX

ᶜAbdallah ibn Saᶜd: 9
Abri-Delgo Reach: 15
Abu Hor: 51, 56, 59
Abu Simbel: 20, 41
Abu Simbel temple: xi, 5
Adendan: 20
Allaqat tribe: 15
American blacks: Nubians compared with, 4, 10, 37
ancestor cults: 34
arable land: xi, 5, 8, 18
arts: 41, 42, 45
assimilation: 3, 12, 43, 45
Aswan: 3, 4, 8, 11, 13, 14, 45, 56
Aswan Dam, first: xii, 5, 36, 46, 49, 50
Aswan High Dam: xi, 3, 5, 6, 7, 16, 17, 20, 41, 50
Asyūt: 13
autochthonous population: Nubians as, 16

Ballana: 12 and n., 18, 20, 23, 41
baraka: 28, 33, 34
Beni Kanz: 9 and n., 14, 19. SEE ALSO Kenuz, the
burial plots: 40, 42
Byzantine Empire: 8, 9

Christianity: in Nubian history, 7, 8, 9, 10, 12, 15, 17, 50
clubs: xi, 35, 39–40, 41, 42, 46
conflict resolution. SEE polity
cooperatives: 41, 42
cotton: 37
cows: 19, 42

Dahmit: 33, 51, 56, 57, 58, 60
Daraw: 13, 50
Dar el-Salam: xii
date palm trees: 8, 18, 19, 20, 21, 22, 28, 31, 42, 43, 45, 49
death ceremonies: 25–26, 40, 46
Derr: 11
diwani: 29, 51

Dongola: xi, 4, 8, 12, 15
Dongolawī: 14, 15

Edfu: 13
Egypt: 5, 8, 9, 10, 12, 13, 16, 41, 45, 46
employment: 37, 38–39, 41
eskalay: 8, 11, 18, 19, 22, 28, 31, 42
Esna: 13, 14
evil eye: 24–25, 28, 49, 51
extended family: 38

Fagirob, the: 21
Farriq: 51, 53, 54, 55
Fatima, Hand of: 24
Fatimid period: 9 n.
Fedija, the: language of, 9, 15; forebears of, 11, 12, 14, 15; houses of, 15, 49, 50–51, 51–56; and *eskalay*, 18; kinship system of, 19, 20–21, 23, 32–33, 35; weddings of, 27–31, 43; clubs of, 39–40, 42

Gaᶜafra: 13, 14
gabila: 32
gamaᶜiyyas. SEE clubs
gold: 29
golden age: 12, 16, 36

Hagana: 13
henna: 28
houses: building materials for, 49–53; southern type, 49–55; decoration of, 50, 53–55, 57–60; northern type, 56–60
Hungarians: 11

Ibn Khaldūn: 9
intermarriage: 4, 9, 11, 12, 14, 15, 32
irrigation: 8, 18, 19, 46
Islam: in Nubian history, 7, 9, 10, 12, 24, 27, 34, 37, 50

Kalabsha: 51, 59
Kanz el-Dawla: 9 n.

karray: 26, 28, 29, 31
Kāshif: Ottoman, 11, 12, 17; of Mohammed Ali regime, 12, 15, 18
Kashim el-Ghurba: 5
keeyay: 18
Kenuz, the: forebears of, 9, 14; language of, 9, 14, 15; slavery and, 10; and Dongolawī, 14; kinship system of, 19–20, 40; saint cult of, 20, 32–35, 43; clubs of, 39–40, 42; houses of, 49, 51, 56–60
Khartoum: 13
kinship system: 18, 19, 20–21, 22, 23, 32–33, 35
Kom Ombo: 3, 5, 13, 14, 43, 45, 46
Kurds: 11
Kush: 13, 16

labor migration: xii, 17, 19, 24, 26, 35, 36–44
languages: 4, 7, 9, 13, 14, 15, 16, 43, 45–46
lineage: 9, 32, 35

Madiq: 56
Mahas, the: 15 and n.
Mamelukes: 10, 11, 12
marriage: 18, 19, 20, 22, 24, 27–31, 42, 43, 46
matrilineal inheritance: 9, 20, 21
medieval Nubia: 7, 10, 14
Meroitic period: 50
migration. SEE labor migration
Mohammed Ali: 10, 12
moulid: 20, 32–35, 42, 43, 46

nakib: 34
names: derivation of, 21
Nasser, Lake: xi, 45, 49
Nasser revolution: 8, 17
natural resources: 4, 8, 12, 17, 20, 22, 26
Nilotic peoples: 4, 9, 16
nog: 20, 21, 25, 28, 31, 40, 41, 42, 43. SEE ALSO kinship system

145

northern Nubians. SEE Kenuz, the
Nubian: term as self-referrent, 15, 16
Nubian Ethnological Survey: xii, 20
Nubians: qualities of, xi, xii, 3, 4, 5, 11,
    17, 19, 22, 26, 39; appearance of, 3, 4,
    13. SEE ALSO polity

omda: 17
Ottoman Turks: 11, 12

Pharaonic period: xi, 3, 5, 7, 14, 50
Philae temple: 11
polity: 5, 17–26, 42
property ownership: 9, 18–19, 28, 30, 31,
    34, 35, 42

Qasr Ibrim: 7, 11, 12
Qustul: 51, 52

Rabīᶜa: 9

religion. SEE Christianity; Islam
resettlement: 3, 5, 13, 17, 26, 42, 43,
    45–46
roofs: flat, 50, 51, 52, 56, 58; vaulted, 50,
    58, 60

Saᶜīdī: 13, 14
saints' shrines: 20, 33, 34
schools: 5, 17, 39, 40, 41, 42, 45
seefa: 29
sharecropping: 36
Shariᶜa law: 30
shrines. SEE saints' shrines
slavery: 4, 8, 9, 10, 12, 36, 38
social clubs. SEE clubs
social organization: xi, 12, 17, 20, 21, 24,
    31, 38, 49
southern Nubians. SEE Fedija, the
Sudan: xi, 4, 12, 13
Sufism: 21

sugar cane: 45
Sukkots, the: 15

Tafa: 58
Theodora, Empress: 8
trade: merchant, 4, 9, 14, 15; tourist, 37
tribal organization: 20, 32, 33, 35, 40
Tushka: 39, 40

urban clubs. SEE clubs

Wadi el-Arab: xii, 15, 50
Wadi Halfa: 14, 15
waṣṭa: 22
water wheel. SEE *eskalay*

X-Group period: 50

Yemama: 9